Aspergers in Love
Couple Relationships and Family Affairs

Maxine Aston

Foreword by Gisela and Chris Slater-Walker

Jessica Kingsley Publishers
London and New York

First published in the United Kingdom in 2003
by Jessica Kingsley Publishers Ltd
116 Pentonville Road
London N1 9JB, England
and
29 West 35th Street, 10th fl.
New York, NY 10001-2299, USA

www.jkp.com

Copyright © Maxine Aston 2003

Library of Congress Cataloging in Publication Data
A CIP catalog record for this book is available from the Library of Congress

British Library Cataloguing in Publication Data
A CIP catalogue record for this book is available from the British Library

ISBN 1 84310 115 7

Printed and Bound in Great Britain by
Athenaeum Press, Gateshead, Tyne and Wear

I see you, and you see me.
I experience you, and you experience me.
I see your behaviour. You see my behaviour.
But I do not and never have and never will see your experience of me.
Just as you cannot 'see' my experience of you.

R.D. Laing
The Politics of Experience and The Bird of Paradise (1967)

Acknowledgements

A huge thank-you to all the couples and individuals who took the time to fill in my questionnaires, allowed me to interview them and shared with me fragments of their private lives. Without you this book would not have been possible. This book is written for you.

Thank you Brenda Wall, Karen Rodman, Roger Meyer, Linda Newland, Chris and Gisela Slater-Walker and, of course, Dr Tony Attwood, for the important roles you have all played in the journey to increase awareness and gain support for families affected by Asperger syndrome.

John Christopher, a special thank-you for the support and encouragement you have given me during the writing of this book and for the time you have spent reading it through and offering me your thoughts.

Carol Darmon for proofreading the initial copy of the manuscript.

David Jones for his knowledge about army tanks.

Dr Mark Forshaw for his inspiring lectures and for offering the quotation that left a lasting impression on me.

My Special Mum and family for being proud of me.

My three children, Zoe, Zara and William for the cups of tea and words of encouragement.

Contents

Foreword

When Chris received his diagnosis in 1997 we were relieved at first, and then we realized that for people in our position, there was very little help available. A parent of a child with Asperger syndrome advised me to 'Read everything you can get your hands on about the subject and then re-read it and re-read it again'. This was very good advice, and it certainly did not take very long to do as she suggested because there was very little at all to read about AS in any form. And what was available did not seem to cover the difficulties of able and apparently independent adults with AS and their partners.

Chris and I estimate that it took around five years, a lot of misunderstanding and eventually writing our own book to feel that we understood Asperger syndrome sufficiently to feel that we had maximized our chances of our marriage succeeding properly despite the communication problems that we encounter. How much easier it would have been if Maxine's books had been available to us in those early days. Fortunately for adults diagnosed today, although there is still little available in the way of professional support, there is more literature available, but much of it is still directed at parents. Whilst this is useful it does not really identify the particular difficulties faced by people with Asperger syndrome and their partners, or provide real guidelines in how these problems can be approached.

We have both known Maxine nearly as long as we have known Chris had Asperger syndrome and have seen her expertise develop and the extent of her research increase. She is the only professional currently working as counsellor and researcher in the field of relationships in which one partner has Asperger syndrome, and so she is uniquely placed to write this book.

People with Asperger syndrome are all linked by the 'triad of impairments' which characterize all autistic spectrum disorders: in social interaction, communication and imagination. These of course are things that would seem to be essential elements of any successful relationship, the ability to understand what the other partner is thinking and to communicate intimately and freely with each other, and so it should be easy to understand why Asperger syndrome poses such a threat to a marriage. Yet a common experience is for people to feel that nobody outside the relationship really does understand. In her book, not only does Maxine make clear the difficulties that both partners in such a relationship experience, she also suggests strategies for dealing with them.

Although people on the autistic spectrum do share certain similarities, that does not mean that they are all the same and Maxine's writing clearly reflects the variety of partners on and off the spectrum that she has encountered. I am sure that there will be people who read the book and find experiences or characteristics with which they are not familiar, but I am sure that there are many more who will read this book and breathe a sigh of relief that there really is someone who does understand the impact of Asperger syndrome on both partners in a 'mixed marriage'.

My own experience of living with someone with Asperger syndrome has convinced me that these relationships can be sustainable and mutually beneficial – given the right two people, a correct diagnosis and supportive family and friends. For many couples, this is not the case, but Aspergers In Love is a very positive step towards increasing the recognition of their problems so that they feel less alone.

Gisela and Chris Slater-Walker

Terminology

Finding the right terminology can be quite difficult in a book like this especially when dealing with a name like Asperger syndrome. The book could rapidly become long-winded, constantly making reference to the person whom has Asperger syndrome and the person who does not have Asperger syndrome.

In order to simplify the script and make life easier for the reader and myself I have used abbreviations when possible. The person with Asperger syndrome will be described as the AS person. The person who does not have Asperger syndrome and so is by definition neuro-typical will be described as the NT person.

The next issue I need to clarify is that because the majority of my samples with Asperger syndrome are male and the majority of the neuro-typical samples are female, I will most of the time refer to the AS partner as male and the NT partner as female. There are sections through-out the book that specifically talk about the female with Asperger syndrome and this will be clearly shown.

Introduction

Just over a year ago I received a phone call from a well-known television presenter who was toying with the idea of having a slot in his programme on Asperger syndrome (AS) and the difficulties it presents in couple relationships. He started by asking a few questions about AS.

'Well, first, what is this Asperger syndrome? I presume it is a mental illness and can be helped with medication – is it curable?'

'Asperger syndrome', I answered, 'is not a mental illness; it is a developmental disorder and it cannot be cured with medication or otherwise.'

'Oh! OK that's interesting,' came the reply. 'Yes – OK, but these people can't love can they? They don't have feelings, so they don't know how to love!'

'Yes, they can love,' I quickly corrected, 'and they do have feelings, but they have difficulty reading other people's feelings. Look, let me explain what Asperger syndrome is and isn't and then I will explain about AS and love.'

So many times I have been asked questions like these, yet it never ceases to surprise me when I discover how little is known about this disorder. Asperger syndrome affects at least one in every two hundred and fifty people. It is thought that the real figure is probably much higher because of the many people who remain undiagnosed.

The very fact that there are so many cases of Asperger syndrome yet to be discovered just highlights the lack of awareness by both public and professionals. So little is understood both from the public point of view and, far more dangerously, by professionals who owe it to the people they come into contact with to understand just what this invisible yet disabling syndrome is all about.

In my previous book *The Other Half of Asperger Syndrome* I wrote about the experience of the adult in an intimate relationship with an Asperger syndrome partner. This was the first self-help book of its kind and offered many strategies that could be used to help the relationship run more smoothly. *Aspergers in Love* is quite different because it also looks at the experience of the person who has Asperger syndrome and it is written about their perspective. It gives the reader a glimpse into what it is like for an adult who has Asperger syndrome, the difficulties that having a relationship can bring and the positive side of the syndrome as well as the problems it can cause. This book also contrasts the perception of the AS person with the perception of their neuro-typical (NT) partners.

It has been said in the past that people with Asperger syndrome do not form intimate relationships, and some do not. This is rarely because the desire for a relationship is not present. It is more likely that a lack of social skills makes it too difficult to build up and maintain a relationship. This is one of the differences between autism and Asperger syndrome. Most people with Asperger syndrome want and need a relationship with another person; those with autism rarely have the same need for people and often find solace in objects instead.

Asperger syndrome causes problems in communication, social interaction and imagination causing a narrow focus and repetitive singular interests. In other words, problems with most of the major qualities needed to form friendships and relationships. Therefore, it is not surprising that when a relationship is formed it will be affected by problems in these areas. When this happens there is often very little support or understanding on offer to the couple from outside sources.

The research for this book came from information provided by forty-one adults with Asperger syndrome, all with current or previous intimate relationships, and by thirty-five of their partners. The adults with AS had either been officially diagnosed or self-diagnosed. Six of the adults with Asperger syndrome were female and they were all in relationships with another adult who had Asperger syndrome or strong autistic traits.

The information gathered came from interviews, questionnaires and case study examples. All names have been changed and any identifying information has been removed, unless permission has been given by the participants to publish their accounts.

This book is therefore written from the perspective of the adult with Asperger syndrome and those who live with them. It gives a voice to the silent minority who struggle every day with the very aspects of humanity that many of us take totally for granted. The person with AS experiences a life-long struggle to understand and interpret a confusing and bewildering world that is full of double meanings, misleading communication and social demands that do not even begin to make sense. Their disability is not visible, it does not affect their intelligence, but the effect the disorder has on their relationships can be devastating. It also affects those who live with them, their partners, their parents and their children. It is a family affair that begs for recognition and support.

This book should dispel some myths, present the facts and offer the reader an understanding and perspective of the world of people with Asperger syndrome and the people that they love.

1

Attraction

In my first book I looked at the core elements that attracted an NT woman to an AS man. Initial attraction seemed to be based on the kind, gentle and quiet manner men with Asperger syndrome can often exhibit. Many of the NT women in my research appeared to be strong, nurturing and with excellent social abilities. From this, it could be assumed that these are the qualities that attracted their partners to them. My latest research has put this to the test.

I asked the AS men what it was that initially attracted them to their partner. Many men based their attraction to a particular woman on how much she was attracted to them. Being liked, approved and needed appeared very important to men with AS. This is not surprising when one looks at the very nature of AS and how it differs from autism.

The world of the autistic adolescent excludes other children and there is often no need to be in the company of other people, to appear popular amongst peers or to be liked by others. Asperger syndrome is very different, and the adolescent often has a very strong desire to be popular and liked. Adolescents want to be part of a group and desperately need to be accepted by those around them. Unfortunately for many AS adolescents, the desire to be popular is present but the social ability to achieve the popularity is not. Communication skills and the capability for successful social interaction are often lacking so, despite many efforts, the adolescent with Asperger syndrome never seems to get it quite right.

I asked one adolescent with AS if he had many friends, to which he replied in the affirmative.

'How do you know they are your friends?' I asked.

'Because they ask me to help them with their homework,' came his reply.

This teenager was an absolute wizard at mathematics and was completely naive to the fact his peers were using him to help them achieve higher grades. This eventually reached a head when three identical pieces of coursework were handed in!

Lack of ability in reading the more subtle facial expressions and body language also make it difficult for the AS adolescent to know when another person is being friendly or sarcastic. One teenager told me that if a girl smiled at him, he would approach her and ask her what she was doing that evening. This came before the normal introductions and building up some sort of rapport. He was, needless to say, given some very frank replies but still used the same chat up line. His eagerness to be liked and accepted caused him endless problems, as his intentions were so often completely misread. This is not uncommon for the AS adolescent, which is why it is important that teachers and professionals are aware of the difficulties that having Asperger syndrome can engender.

For the AS adult, the need to be liked and accepted still exists and it is often the NT woman who makes the first move or shows him quite clearly that she is attracted to him. It might be that she simply smiles at him, or strikes up a conversation with him that will have given him the signal that she likes him. The way a prospective partner makes him feel and fits into his world is often paramount in whether the relationship will progress. It is her attraction to him that often becomes his attraction to her.

Physical attraction rather than sexual attraction also plays an important role in the AS agenda and it appears to be a specific aspect of the partner's appearance that catches his interest. In my research, hair and eyes were highest on the preference list. Asperger syndrome produces a very narrow focus and rather than seeing the complete person, a specific part of her face or body may be the attraction. Sexual attraction was rarely mentioned and did not seem very high on the list of requirements. Only one man mentioned breasts, and another talked about bottoms. Legs did not get a look in! This may explain why many women say that part of their initial attraction to their AS partner was that he was such a gentleman and his intentions did not appear to be sexual. This can be very appealing and refreshing especially if a woman has a history of over-eager men who might have made her feel that her attraction was purely sexual. It can come as quite a relief to feel at ease and comfortable with a man who is gentle and attentive and she will often see this as a sign of respect for her. However, it is quite likely that this is because having sex with her is not top of his list of priorities and he is more interested in how well she fits into his world and how well they are matched academically.

In some cases Asperger syndrome can produce heightened sensory perception, and the senses may be very attuned to external stimulation. It may be sensitivity to light, or particular smells or certain fabrics. This may also play a part in partner choice. One man was able instantly to recognize the perfume a woman wore; he had the most amazing sense and memory for smell. He had favourites, and it was very important to him that his partner wore the right perfume. He made sure of this by buying her perfumes and bath oils quite early in the relationship. His girlfriend interpreted this as generosity whereas, in fact, he was ensuring that his needs were satisfied. Needless to say, it was almost certain that to please him she would wear the perfume! On the other hand, this man could also be very honest in his opinion of a person's body odour and told one date that she smelt of body odour! As can be imagined, the relationship ended there.

These likes and dislikes can be very rigid: if an AS man likes long hair it is unlikely he would find a woman with short hair attractive. If a woman he meets does not quite meet his criteria, he may try to mould her into his ideal partner. It is conceivable that he has very rigid definitions of femininity, perhaps originating with his mother or even someone he has seen on television. His idea of being feminine might require, for instance, that the woman has long nails, and he will actively encourage his new partner to grow and maintain long manicured nails. This could be via praise of her, or by telling her of a previous girlfriend with beautiful nails. Or it may be directed at her in a very critical and hurtful way such as showing disappointment if she does not come up to his expectations.

One man liked his partner to wear stockings, which she found not always comfortable. When she refused to wear them to take the dog for a walk in the park, he informed her that he was very disappointed in her behaviour and took it very personally. He could not understand that it was about the practicality of the situation and not personal spite.

Many AS men have a history of being rejected and bullied, so when he meets a woman who meets the necessary criteria for wife or partner he will make every effort to impress her and make her happy. He will focus all his attention on her and make her feel very special indeed. Many women describe this courtship time as a happy and a special time in the relationship, which unfortunately often comes to an abrupt end once the relationship is sealed. At this time many NT women are left disillusioned and wondering how they got it all so wrong that they did not see their partner's true character.

It does appear though that it is not only the women who are left feeling like this, as their AS partners describe a similar feeling. They use terms like 'she seemed to like me', 'she seemed to be good fun' or 'she seemed to be gentle'. This is said in a way that indicates they are also feeling that they got it wrong! If both partners in the relationship are left feeling as though they were deceived into believing their partner was different from their current behaviour, they could become equally resentful and both will stop giving and trying to please the other. This can have a very destructive effect on both partners and when the NT partner tries to explain why she is reacting differently, it is often misunderstood by the AS partner. He may have difficulty realizing that when he gave her so much attention and care, she was happy and went out of her way to please him. However, when he suddenly stopped putting in any effort into the relationship after they moved in together, she became unhappy and reacted against this.

This is due to the lack of imaginative thought which occurs in Asperger syndrome and results in the AS person not being able to see the consequences of his actions. He very often does not make the link between his behaviour and her reaction. He does not realize that if he shows her the same love and attention he did in the beginning, she will probably reciprocate his affection.

The views of AS women about attraction are very similar to those of AS men. Physical attraction is limited to a particular feature and, once again, it is hair and eyes that are particularly mentioned. Some women were attracted by the sense of authority a man offered, being mature or a father figure. All the men were older than the women, sometimes by many years. (This age difference also appears to affect AS men, as many are in relationships with an older woman.)

Another similarity between AS men and women is that their attraction depends very much on how much the potential partner likes them. One woman said quite categorically that she never did like her partner when they met and they only married because he was so attracted to her and was persistent. She said he mistook her friendliness as a sign that she was attracted to him, when in fact this was very far removed from the truth.

In summary, adults with AS are initially attracted to a potential partner because the potential partner shows that they like them and appears to offer them acceptance. Physical attraction seems to depend on a particular feature of the person, for example, eyes, and, finally, the attraction is unlikely to be entirely a sexual one.

The next most important factor in whether the relationship progresses is whether their potential partner has similar interests to theirs.

Key points

- An AS man often bases his attraction to a particular woman on how much she is attracted to him.
- Physical attraction is more relevant than sexual attraction in partner choice by both men and women with AS.
- Hair and eyes are the most frequently mentioned and desirable physical attributes of the chosen NT partner.
- Sensitivity to smell or particular fabrics was apparent for some AS men.
- The likes and dislikes held by the AS male can be very rigid.
- Initially, the AS male may do everything possible to make his new partner feel special and happy.

- Later in the relationship both partners are sometimes left feeling that 'they got it all wrong'.
- AS men and women described the reasons they were attracted to their chosen partner in very similar ways.

2

Shared Interests

Special interests can form an integral part of Asperger syndrome and therefore it is not surprising to discover that choice of partner is very often strongly linked to shared interests. These similarities do not just include activities and hobbies, but also beliefs, standards and attitudes.

Love of music is very important and was the most frequently cited shared interest. This was not always just listening to music, but also musical talent and ability. Appreciation by both partners of the same music rates very highly. Music can be very mood changing and can offer a temporary escape from the stresses of life. It is therapeutic and the mind can be totally absorbed by it; it appears to play an essential role for many AS adults. Another plus about listening to music together is that there is no need to talk at the same time. Music is about listening, not talking and can form a very important part of relaxing and winding down; it can offer a useful distraction when anxiety is high.

The love of music may be linked to the heightened sensory perception that is often associated with Asperger syndrome, and sounds can either enhance relaxation or provoke stress and frustration. Sensitivity to certain sounds, pitches and notes are likely to be responsible for this. High-pitched sounds and indeed voices seem to grate with AS children and adults just like chalk on a blackboard. One AS man threatened his neighbour that if he did not stop his dog barking he would take action to make the dog quiet. The dog's bark was very high-pitched and caused him quite severe stress and anxiety.

Second on the list is the theatre. The theatre, like music, can offer an escape from reality and all the stresses of day-to-day living. It is a chance to 'people watch' and observe how others behave. Because of the problems in social interaction, many people with AS often learn to role-play by observing other people. This may be from real life, television, cinema or theatre, and it is not uncommon to adopt certain habits, expressions or even accents that have been observed in others. The other bonus about going to the theatre or to watch a show together is that the audience is not expected to converse all the way through it.

A shared interest in the arts, whether music, opera, art or theatre, seems likely to exist between a couple when one partner has Asperger syndrome. For others it may be dining out or maybe just sharing a take-away together.

History is another interest that may be shared; it could be the royal family, a particular era or building and architecture. One man discussed with enthusiasm how he and his partner shared an interest in eighteenth-century architecture and would arrange days out and weekends away that would allow them to visit and explore different historical buildings.

Not many couples shared sporting interests; walking was mentioned by two couples. Love of animals, especially cats, was shared by at least six of the couples I contacted. Being independent, often solitary creatures, cats make few demands beyond being fed, and can be affectionate without being overly demonstrative. Maybe there is something about the nature of cats that is appealing to a selection of people with Asperger syndrome. One person once told me that his cat was the only real love in his life, and the only living creature he felt he could relate to.

Shared beliefs were highlighted by many as being very important in partner choice, especially spiritual beliefs. Many of the men talked about their shared religious beliefs and for most their commitment to their chosen faith was paramount. Religion offers very clear-cut rules and rituals. There is often a right way and a wrong way, with little or no deviation between. This can feel quite comfortable for the person with AS because it offers clear directions that can be easily followed. It also implies safety, in the hope that a person with strong religious beliefs will be honest and loyal. If partners share these fundamental beliefs it can be seen to offer more safety and security to the relationship and remove a proportion of the risk and guesswork that the AS person has to make to evaluate his potential partner's moral beliefs and trustworthiness.

It seems that most of the women chosen by AS men have very strong values, morals and beliefs. They are committed in their beliefs, and hence often committed in their relationship. This is not always the case however. On the other side of the coin, one couple was attracted to each other's atheism and 'not believing' formed an important part of their relationship.

Almost half the men I contacted stated that a shared sense of humour was important to them. One man was attracted to the fact his partner laughed at his jokes. This once again reflects on childhood and the boyish quality that a few men with AS have. The Asperger sense of humour can be quite adolescent in its approach. The problem is that when the AS person discovers a good joke or a way to make someone laugh they can go into overkill, not realizing that the joke is only funny once. It could be said that the NT partner's sense of humour plays an essential part in keeping the relationship together. There will be many times when seeing the funny side of an embarrassing situation will help save the day.

Other areas stated to be important by AS men were having shared political and ethical beliefs. A desire for family life was also expressed as important and the particular women they had formed relationships with also sought the distinct roles and security it offered.

The women with AS had similar feelings to the AS men; music, the theatre or religious beliefs were also very important to them. Others felt it was important to be matched on an intellectual level and wanted someone they could converse with. They were perhaps more aware of their chosen partner's faults than the AS men were and appreciated that they were not going to get everything they wanted. This may be due to gender differences in upbringing, not AS, as girls are still generally reared to make allowances for male behaviour. For example, boys are often given more freedom and allowances are often made for boisterous or uncouth be-haviour that would be less tolerated in girls.

In summary, the AS man wants someone who can share his interests and the most common interests stated were music and the theatre. He wants someone who will do things with him, but it is unlikely he will choose someone with specific interests that he will have to learn to join in with. She will have to complement him and may sometimes find herself giving up the things she likes doing in order to accommodate his needs. This might work for a while but could cause resentment later on in the relationship when these sacrifices are not reciprocated or appreciated.

It appears that it is safe, secure, caring and committed women who are top of the list of choice of partner and this is far more important than sexual attraction or popularity. He relies on her qualities to compensate for what he cannot instinctively sense. He needs to know by her attitudes and life-style that she is safe because he cannot read it in her nature. He needs to know if he can trust and rely on her to be honest and faithful to him.

Key points

- Shared interests is an important deciding factor in partner choice by the AS man and woman.
- Love of music is the most common shared interest.
- Love of the theatre is the second most common shared interest.
- Sporting activities are the least common shared interest.
- The couples sometimes share a love of animals, particularly cats.
- Shared beliefs, especially spiritual beliefs, are very important in partner choice.
- AS men often choose women with strong values, morals and beliefs.
- The majority of AS men say their partners' sense of humour is important to them.
- AS women rank music, theatre, religious beliefs and intellectual ability as being important shared interests with their chosen partner.
- AS women show a greater awareness of their partners' faults than AS men and also recognize that they are not going to get everything they want.

3

Trust

Knowing he can trust his partner is vital to many AS men. Trust needed to be established quite early on, and this was often achieved by evaluating the woman's morals and beliefs. But how well does this trust last and is it reciprocated?

Seventy-five per cent of the AS men stated they had complete or, almost complete, trust in their partner and this was regardless of how long the relationship had been going on. In a few cases, the relationships had lasted over forty years. These feelings were expressed by terms like 'I trust her implicitly' 'I trust her one hundred per cent', 'I have implicit trust in my partner in all areas'. The trust offered by most of these men was almost childlike and naive.

This vulnerability is often apparent in children and adolescents with Asperger syndrome. Part of the reason for this is that due to the inability to put themselves into another's mind, and see another's motives, they cannot always figure out when they are being lied to or used. This can make children prime targets for those who abuse that trust and they can find themselves at times in serious trouble because they just did what they were told. One young man was at a party when a so-called mate offered him drugs. This 'friend' knew that he was against drugs so for a laugh told him it was candy, he believed his 'friend' and took one. The pills were Ecstasy and the young man was soon in a state of total panic and lost control. He had to be taken to hospital; the police were involved and did not believe that he really thought it was candy. The whole episode caused a lot of grief for both the boy and his parents.

It is very easy to lie to someone with Asperger syndrome and other children and adolescents may realize this quite quickly. The AS person cannot read the non-verbal signals that often give people away when they are lying or being deceitful, they do not always understand when someone is being sarcastic and may take things very literally. They need extra protection against this and this is why early intervention and support can make so much difference to growing up with Asperger syndrome.

The AS adult may be more cautious, probably having learnt from a lifetime of mistakes and getting caught out. This is conceivably why he may take his time to feel assured that his chosen partner is, in his eyes, honest and trustworthy. Once he has made this decision about her, it does not change, unless she does something very blatant and deceitful.

Almost all the men expressed complete trust in their partner's fidelity, though two had discovered their partners had had an affair and their trust for these women was completely shattered. For one of these men the relationship with his partner had ended and he had met someone else, his trust for his new partner was as total as it had been for the first partner before she deceived him. The previous deceit was completely left behind and no lesson had been learned from it. Just as this can have its benefits it can also cause problems; there often seems to be a failure to learn from experience in Asperger syndrome.

When the AS partner was asked whether they thought their partner trusted them, only one said they did. Within this section of my research many of the men showed deep remorse and sadness at not being trusted, and many blamed themselves for having let their partner down. One man stated that he had completely let his wife down and felt he was quite useless. Many of the men I have come into contact with, did try very hard to please their partner and get it right. Unfortunately, due to the features of Asperger syndrome, these attempts sometimes fail.

One man arranged to take his wife out to a new seafood restaurant that had opened in the city as a surprise treat for her birthday. He told her to put on her best dress and be ready by eight p.m. She was very excited and dressed up for the occasion. Eight p.m., then nine p.m. came and went. She was anxious, worried and disappointed. Meanwhile her husband had been into town to buy her earrings and a card, and on returning to his car realized he had lost his car park ticket. He searched the car, searched himself, and retraced his steps back to the card shop… No ticket! Time was quickly running out and he was getting more and more anxious. He went back to the car park kiosk and despite his explanation was told he would have to pay for twenty-four hours.

By now he was very stressed and becoming quite desperate, unable to see the justification in paying for something he did not owe, and unable to understand that the car park attendant did not automatically know he was telling the truth. Bursting point was reached; he lost his temper and hit the glass on the kiosk window, and unfortunately for him it broke! His cuts were minor but the car park attendant's reaction was not; the police were called and he was arrested for criminal damage.

It was only when his wife had a call from the police station that she knew he was safe. Her reaction when she saw him was one of anger; he had let her down again. Her trust for him had received yet another knock.

Situations like this are not uncommon in AS relationships. The Asperger world can be very 'black and white'. This way of thinking is caused by the inability to put oneself in another's place, known as 'theory of mind'. Theory of mind is being able to enter into another person's mental state and see the world from their perspective. In autism theory of mind is severely affected and some autistic children and adults find it impossible to view anything from a perspective other than their own. Theory of mind is also affected in Asperger syndrome to a lesser degree but the problems it causes can still be serious. In the example shown, the husband's anger was very much directed at the car park attendant and was a result of utter frustration at trying to make him accept that he was being told the truth. He could not see that it was impossible for the car park attendant to know and comprehend something he had no personal experience of.

Not being able to deal with particular situations and people, especially crisis situations, is felt by some AS men as the primary reason their partner did not trust them. Sensory overload is often responsible for this. Trying to cope with too many external pressures at the same time is very stressful and difficult for people with AS. The response may be loss of temper but could also be complete shutdown or withdrawal from the situation. Both withdrawing and explosive behaviour are an attempt by the person to regain control of the situation.

A few AS men mentioned that they felt their partners' trust in them had strengthened since they had received a diagnosis, although this opinion was not echoed in the most of the reports sent in by their wives or partners. Only one woman said she trusted her husband totally and that trust had increased since his diagnosis. She was part of a young couple who had received a diagnosis and appropriate counselling quite early in their relationship.

It is very difficult to have trust in an area one does not understand. The behaviour of people with Asperger syndrome can be very hard to understand. If the NT partner has little or no awareness and knowledge of AS she will continually receive the wrong messages and form a false perception on why some of the things he does make no sense whatsoever and just appear cruel and callous. It is almost impossible to understand this complex and confusing condition without any knowledge of its effects. Awareness in both partners is essential.

In many of the women's replies there was an edge of desperation and issues of trust were no exception. Many women felt they could not trust their AS partner or rely on him for anything: money, talking, looking after the children, being honest, offering emotional support or being responsible. It was even felt by some women that their partners were an actual risk and danger to the family. One woman related how one night she had felt ill and gone to bed early leaving her husband to sort out downstairs and lock up. He said he was going to watch TV for a while and then come up. A little later he came upstairs, got into bed, turned the light out and went to sleep. Quite soon afterwards explosions downstairs awakened them. Despite feeling ill she flew out of bed and ran downstairs into the kitchen. There on the cooker was a black saucepan expelling thick gray smoke. The entire kitchen was splattered in bits of very hard-boiled eggs. He had put his eggs on to boil for his sandwiches, thinking he would save time in the morning, forgotten and then gone to bed.

Not all, but some, men with AS can be quite forgetful and absent-minded. Sometimes this is because they have a pre-recorded script for a particular job or routine and if this is changed or interrupted, aspects can be forgotten. It was not usual for this man to boil his eggs at night; it was a job normally performed by his wife, but he had heard her complain that there was nothing stopping him from doing it, so he thought he would do it himself. It was not in his script and he had reverted back to his normal routine, gone to bed and completely forgotten the eggs.

Almost all NT women trusted their AS partners to be faithful. For a few, this was the only area in which they had any trust and that was very high throughout. Most of the AS men were quite aware that their partner trusted them to be faithful, because that is what she had told him. Many men with AS seemed to value themselves according to what their partner told them.

The AS women gave quite similar answers on the subject of trust. On the whole they trusted their partners; the only area where they expressed any doubts was in the faithfulness of their partners, which was the biggest difference between the AS women and NT women. Nearly all were in some ways suspicious of their partner, although one AS woman said her partner, who also had AS, did not have the skills or ability to be unfaithful to her. Her trust for him was based on this, rather than the knowledge that he wanted to be faithful.

One of the reasons for this difference may be what the AS women learned about men from adolescence. It might have seemed that many teenage boys around them had sex on the top of their priority list. Adolescent boys are often under pressure to show they can score and it is often the boy who is most popular with the girls who will gain respect and be looked up to by others. Girls with AS will be very aware that sex is on the minds of most boys and will probably have had boys make advances to them. This message from adolescence seems to be carried forward into adult relationships and many women may think that if the chance arises to be unfaithful her partner may take it.

Key points

- Almost all the AS men say they have complete trust in their partners.

- This trust appears to be quite naive and childlike.

- The majority of AS men have complete, or almost complete, trust in their partners' fidelity.

- If the NT partner is unfaithful, it is unlikely they will be trusted again.

- It is unusual for an AS man to believe that his NT partner trusts him.

- Not being able to deal with particular situations, people or crises, is the primary reason given by AS men as to why they believe their partners do not trust them.

- It is unusual for an NT woman to totally trust her AS partner.

- The majority of NT women say that they could not trust their partner or rely on him for anything except to be faithful.

- The AS women say they trust their partners in most things, but not to be faithful.

4

Being Valued

The self-esteem of the majority of AS men is particularly low. Many feel quite worthless and of little value to their partners. Statements like 'I am only valued for the jobs I do', 'I am only valued because I bring home a salary' and 'only valued as a provider' are not uncommon.

Most of the NT women are unaware that their partner feels so low, because he does not give her any indication that this is the way he feels. Internalizing feelings and not disclosing being unhappy or stressed seems quite common in both adults and children with Asperger syndrome. This may be especially relevant when there have been past problems with bullying.

Being bullied or teased at school has been disclosed by many adults with AS. The bullying was not usually reported and the suffering went on in silence. When the negative feelings that result are kept hidden, they can develop into depression and the consequence is very low self-esteem and feelings of worthlessness.

One man said he was totally and utterly worthless, he felt he had failed his wife in every conceivable way, lost his job, got things wrong with the kids and then to top it all he had forgotten their wedding anniversary. Although his wife had supported him throughout with encouragement and praise for how hard he had been trying to put things right, he did not appear to hear anything positive she said. I asked him if he had heard her when she said she knew he tried his best and he said he had. I then asked if he valued her opinion, which he affirmed, but then continued to argue that he could not believe what she said if he knew that he was the cause of all the problems.

This is the black and white world of Asperger syndrome. The AS partner may believe he is all bad and useless at relationships, or he may deny what his NT partner is saying and put the blame on her. Which one of these routes he takes will depend on the type of person he is and how his NT partner deals with the problems that arise. This can be very difficult when it is not known that Asperger syndrome is the cause. Although things may improve when Asperger syndrome is discovered, if too much damage has already been done the AS person may stay locked in a very self-destructive world, only hearing the negative things that are said about him.

This happened in the case I described above, and no matter how his wife tried to improve things, the damage had already been done. This man was unable to believe that his wife could see him in any other way than the way he had now come to perceive himself. This is why early intervention and understanding of Asperger syndrome are so important. Once the AS person understands and accepts the syndrome he is then able to see what his abilities are, and also come to understand how many of his disabilities are not his fault.

When I asked AS men 'do you feel valued?' their replies indicated that they evaluate themselves in the relationship according to what their partner tells them. Here is a conversation I had with one man.

Interviewer:	Are you good at doing jobs in the home?
AS:	Yes.
Interviewer:	What in particular?
AS:	My wife has told me that I am good at cutting the grass.
Interviewer:	Do you think you are?
AS:	Well, I must be, because that is what she told me.
Interviewer:	But what is your opinion?
AS:	Yes, I am good at it because I'm good at getting the lines straight.

Later I asked the same man if he thought he could make his wife happy.

AS: No, I can't because she is always telling me how
               unhappy I make her.

Interviewer: But do you want to make her happy?

AS: Yes, but whatever I do I seem to get it wrong
               because she is still unhappy and tells me I do not
               know how to make her happy. I do not bother
               trying anymore.

Cutting the grass is logical and practical and is an area in which a person with Asperger syndrome is quite at home; it does not require any social interaction, communication or imagination. He knew the lines were straight so he knew he was good at cutting the grass. However when it came to the relationship he did not know if he was getting it right because he did not have the natural ability to understand what he was supposed to do. He only had his partner's voiced opinion of him to base himself on.

This man had heard so many times how he had failed at meeting his wife's emotional needs that he had stopped trying. This is known as a self-fulfilling prophecy. A long- term negative way of thinking can change how hard we try, and may eventually mean that, because we believe we will fail, we do not try at all. By the time the majority of us reach adulthood, we will normally have developed a sense of self and the capabilities we have. If we are criticized we can evaluate that criticism according to who said it and why, and the context it was said in. For example, if we are told we are not honest, we will think about why the person has said it and decide if it is true or if it is a biased comment. We also evaluate whether it was perhaps true on this occasion and we were not honest, or perhaps it may have been a white lie to prevent hurting someone. We will evaluate the comment from different perspectives.

Most AS men have a very different way of evaluating what their partners say about them, and it appears that they rarely evaluate their partner's comments in the context that they are made. This is especially true if the man with AS has already decided what was good about himself and what was not, a process that may have occurred quite early in the relationship. If, for example, his partner says that he has been thoughtless, he will only consider the word 'thoughtless', and not the context in which it was said. If he considers himself thoughtless then this will simply reinforce his belief about himself. If however, he has already decided that he is a thoughtful person, then what she is saying will be seen purely as criticism, or as her being vindictive or malicious.

It is no wonder there are so many misunderstandings between partners and that so often the AS person will accuse his partner of continually criticizing him. The self-evaluation that he has already formulated can be very hard to change, and in some cases, it is very dependent on how seriously affected the person is by Asperger syndrome and how able he is to change his thought patterns and broaden his focus.

Half of the men said they only felt valued for what they did or contributed financially, in other words for the logical and practical things that they did. Some took this further to say they felt completely used by their partners; others said they were used to buy things, others felt used for their brains, a few even felt used for sex. Some felt unappreciated for any of the qualities they had and said that they had tried hard to be unselfish and do things for their wives. They told me about the things they had done for their wives that had been very difficult for them.

One man explained how he knew his wife disliked him working nights because she would be on her own. He enjoyed working nights as he was left to his own devices and found this less stressful. He decided to change to days for her sake and timed it for their wedding anniversary. He went to a lot of trouble to do this, but did not tell her that he had done it just for her. His wife was pleased he was going onto days, but had no idea why he was doing it. With the extra work of filling in new contracts and working out his salary, he forgot to get her an anniversary card. She was very upset, told him he did not care about her and that he had let her down again and was totally thoughtless. The word 'thoughtless' was what he heard above anything else, and he felt it was totally unjustified. It had not occurred to him to tell her what he had so unselfishly and thoughtfully done for her, he just presumed she would know. He felt under attack and reacted by retreating, unable to deal with her anger, not knowing what to do to put it right. The situation escalated and he took off in his car, not returning until late. The anniversary was ruined and both felt undervalued.

This kind of misunderstanding is all too common in Asperger relationships, which really do require a different way of thinking.

Sixty per cent of the NT women felt the same as their AS partners, that they were valued in some ways, but not always in the way they would like to be. They felt valued for the way they cared for the family, cooked the meals and looked after their partner's needs. Some felt they were required more to help provide their partner's physical needs than his emotional needs. They felt valued for the caring and nurturing they provided, but this was very similar to the way a mother is needed by a child who has not yet learned to value her for who she is rather than for what she has to offer.

One woman talked about how hard her partner tried to make her happy and how much he valued her, but this did not make her feel good because she did not feel valued for who she was. Most of us wish to be valued for our thoughtfulness, compassion and empathy, and want to be understood by our partner. We would like to know that if we needed some emotional support and assurance it would be offered to us automatically, without us having to ask. Asperger syndrome affects the ability to read the more subtle signs of non-verbal language, and unless an AS man is told directly that his partner has this emotional need he will not be aware of it.

He will not be aware of her need to be praised or acknowledged for the hard work, consideration and self-sacrifice she puts into the relationship. If he thanked her last time she mentioned this to him, he will see no need to say it again. He is not constantly asking her to acknowledge him in what he does, so does not see why she needs him to acknowledge her. She may also think she has little to thank or praise him for as he never reciprocates her emotional caring and the empathy she shows him. If this pattern of behaviour is not broken or brought into the couple's awareness it will soon start to have a very negative effect on both partners. Both will feel they are not valued in the relationship. He will be making his contributions in a practical and active way and she may not be aware that they are his way of saying he cares. His deeds will carry the same value for him as her emotional input does to her. Unfortunately both may go unnoticed and will seem just taken for granted. This creates a lot of disharmony for the couple and both feel unvalued for the qualities they feel they offer.

In one way or another all the AS women felt valued by their partners, but once again not for the things that they felt were important to them.

One area in which they felt very undervalued was their intelligence and independence; another area was their special interests. None of them said they needed to be valued because of their emotional input in the relationship. This was the opposite of the replies by the NT women, which indicates that this is a direct consequence of having Asperger syndrome.

Independence and autonomy are very important to AS women, far more than it appeared to be for AS men, many of whom are happy to hand over the responsibilities of running the home to their partners. AS women say that they wanted to be valued for the way they can take care of themselves. They are capable, hard working and very independent women who need to feel in control of their environments. They see these traits as very positive qualities that are not always appreciated by their partners. This may indicate a difference in gender expectations and may relate to the changes to women's role in society. All the AS women in my research were aged between forty and sixty-five, they had faced many changes in the female role and now perhaps felt more able to exercise control and power over their status in the relationship than they had in the past.

Key points

- The self-esteem of most AS men appears to be very low.
- Many AS men evaluate themselves in a relationship according to what their partner tells them.
- Sometimes the AS man will stop trying altogether because he believes he will always fail.
- AS men rarely evaluate their partners comments within the context in which they are said.
- Half of AS men say they only feel valued for what they contribute to the household financially or practically.
- The majority of NT partners only feel valued for what they do, rather than who they are.

- All of the AS women feel valued by their partners in some way, but not for the things that were important to them.
- All the AS women would like to be valued for their independence, intelligence or autonomy.

5

Understanding

When I asked whether the AS man felt he understood his partner there was a very mixed reaction, some of the men felt they completely understood their partner, seventy-eight per cent felt they understood certain aspects of her. Only four felt they did not understand her at all. One man struggled very hard with this question and argued that it would be impossible to ever understand someone else's mind, when it could not be entered or read by anyone but the owner. He continued to say that he could only understand what he could observe, and as he could not observe his wife's thought patterns he would never be able to understand her.

For one person to be able to understand another requires empathy, it requires that you can put yourself in their shoes and understand what they think and how they feel. Lack of empathy is said to be symptomatic of AS; this gives the impression that the person with Asperger syndrome does not have any feelings. This is not the case! Many men said that they could understand and therefore empathise with their wives to a lesser or greater extent. Only two men stated they could not understand her at all. If the criteria of Asperger syndrome states this cannot happen, what is going on when these men argue that they can understand their partners?

I asked one man if he understood his wife.

'Yes,' he said, 'we have gone through so much to try and make this relationship work, that I know I understand her very well.'

'That must make life much easier for you, because you would know what she wanted from you.'

'Oh no!' he said. 'It has been very stressful lately.'

'Why is that?' I asked.

'Because I never know how she is going to react, sometimes she can get quite angry with me for no reason.'

'But surely if you understand your wife you will know why she is upset or angry?' I enquired further.

'Yes, I know why she does this; it is because she can then feel better about herself, if she puts me down.'

'Can you think of an example?' I asked him.

'Yes,' he replied, 'my wife works late on a Wednesday so I normally cook supper for both of us. I had had quite a heavy business lunch and was not hungry so I did not bother to cook anything and went to the gym instead; she has said I need to lose weight. I thought she would be pleased.'

'So what did happen?' I asked.

'She was very upset and criticized me for not cooking supper. She said she would not have done that to me. She was putting me down so she could feel better. I just never know what she wants me to do.' He looked at me in total bewilderment.

Looking into this statement more deeply, it becomes apparent that this is a person with Asperger syndrome trying to make sense of what was going on around him. He could not relate her reaction to his actions; he was unable to see that it was what he did that made her angry and upset. It was his turn to do something for her, he was not hungry, and he remembered she wanted him to lose weight. It had not occurred to him that she had worked a long day and wanted to come home, eat and relax. He had seen things only from an introspective point of view. He had at some point in the past already decided that she put him down purely to feel better about herself, and then applied this conclusion to this situation and to every time something went wrong and she was upset.

Having Asperger syndrome disables the ability to predict the con-sequences of one's actions to someone else, especially in different contexts or situations. For example, one woman had asked her husband if he would come straight home after work for his tea and not go straight to the gym. His continual going to the gym had caused problems as she felt he was doing this in order to avoid spending time with the children and helping her with the chores. He kept his word, did not go to the gym and everything was fine until one evening he did not come home till late. She asked where he had been and he said to the gym. She reminded him that they had agreed he should come straight home from work; he explained his colleague at work had asked if he would show him around the gym after work and he had done just that. Because the situation was different and he was going there with a friend, he presumed that she would be OK about it and there was no need to let her know. It was as though he had presumed she would know what he was doing and understand, because he knew what he was doing and the reason he had not come home first.

I have been asked many times in the counselling room by AS men to just tell them what to do to make their wives happy, because they really do not know. This plea is very genuine. One man, who had said that he understood his wife's needs, explained that he understood her need for him to be intimate, her need for him to make her feel special and her need to be emotionally supported. He had no problem understanding this is what she needed, but then he said quite desperately, 'trouble is I do not know how it is possible to fulfil these needs'. It is like understanding that someone needs to be fed, but not having a clue what to feed him or her and not having any food to offer. The practical side of the need is understood, but the feelings and emotions that are required to fulfil the need are not available. This man also said his partner wanted him to be perfect and he realized from her criticism how far from perfect he must be. Most of the men I have spoken to do try to understand their wives but, as one man said, he can only understand what she tells him. If he is not told what she thinks or wants he will fill in the gaps himself and, unfortunately, may come to the wrong conclusions.

Rita Carter, in her book *Mapping the Mind*, says that those with Aspergers syndrome use a different region in the brain to work out problems that require theory of mind. She found that when NT people are-read a story that involves inferring someone else's state of mind, the left medial prefrontal cortex lights up on brain scans. This is the part of the brain that is responsible for intuitive and insightful thinking.

When the same story is read to someone who has Asperger syndrome, brain scans show that a different part of the brain becomes active. The area activated in the AS brain is the area used for logical and straightforward problems, used by those with and without Asperger syndrome to work out practical things.

This explains why it often takes someone with AS longer to work out a problem that demands some insight. It also explains why so often the wrong conclusion will be reached – instead of automatically knowing why their partner has reacted in a certain way, it is reasoned out in a logical way. This is probably the reason that so many women end up frustrated and upset trying to explain to their partners that they do not always want a practical and logical solution to what is bothering them. They want their partners to intuitively know and understand what is required of them. They want to feel their partners understand their needs and desires without having to spell it out to them time after time.

One woman complained to her husband that he never spoke to her during their lovemaking and said that it would be really good if he could express romantic and heartfelt feelings for her. Next time they made love and she asked her husband to say something nice to her, he responded by telling her that he thought she was a very good cook!

Examples like this are not uncommon and can leave the NT partner feeling very misunderstood and undervalued. It is, however, not possible for the AS partner to respond in any other way, though he can learn to say and do certain things that will make her feel happier. He can learn for instance that hugs, kisses and a hand to hold are often more comforting to her than rushing off to make her a cup of tea, and then leaving her to drink it on her own.

Men with AS will often try to solve emotional problems by finding a practical solution, not understanding that this is often the last thing their partner wants. This is not deliberate and is a consequence of having to work with a different part of the brain than an NT person would use. AS men do not have the benefit of natural intuition and insightful thought and have to rely purely on logical and factual thought to work out what their partner wants from them. This is quite a difficult concept to understand, but it is vital that the NT partner does understand that this disability is caused by AS, otherwise she will be left feeling he has purposely ignored her needs and not even bothered to try to understand her.

There are times within my counselling when I will see couples at the very beginning of their journey to the discovery of Asperger syndrome. In the case of a few couples I have seen, there is no awareness that AS is causing the problems they have. They are aware that something is wrong and I am often told by a very desperate and frustrated NT partner that she knows he cares about her, knows he is doing his best, so why is he so damned selfish? Why does he say he will change and then not? Why doesn't he understand what she is trying to tell him? Why doesn't he understand her and her needs? How can he say he loves her yet be so insensitive and cruel? Why can't he discuss emotions? It is not surprising that many of these women come to see me saying the same things, feeling the same way and sometimes doubting their own sanity. Meanwhile her partner will be sitting beside her saying very little, if anything at all, and with no idea why she is always so upset with him.

Later, when it is revealed that AS may be the cause of the problems and perhaps a diagnosis is sought and confirmed, then and only then is the NT partner able to begin to make sense of and understand what has been going so wrong in their relationship. The relief this can bring for both partners is tremendous. This is the point when her understanding of him begins, and often the point when he is able to understand himself better and become more aware of what his partner has been saying to him for so many years.

The women with AS felt they did understand their partner up to a point and had learned to understand many of his ways. It was, however, also very important to them that he should understand her. Some of the AS women felt confused that although their partners appeared to understand them, they would sometimes go and do something that showed they clearly did not. One AS woman explained this by the fact that her partner also had Asperger syndrome and this made him do strange things.

Key points

- The majority of AS adults believe they understand certain aspects of their partners.
- Asperger syndrome disables the ability to predict the consequences of one's actions on someone else.

- In *Mapping the Mind* Rita Carter states that people with AS use a different region of the brain from NT individuals to work out problems involving theory of mind.

- AS adults do not have the benefit of natural intuition and insightful thought.

- The majority of NT partners feel their understanding of their AS partners had increased since the diagnosis of Asperger syndrome.

- AS women feel they can understand their partners up to a point.

- It is important to AS women that their partners understand them.

6

Self-disclosure

Being open and honest with one's chosen partner is essential if a natural and trustful bonding is going to be achieved. I asked the AS men in my study whether they felt able to be open and disclose information to their partners.

Although sixty-nine per cent of AS men said they could make some disclosures to their partners, only ten per cent felt they were able to disclose information regarding themselves. This is quite a contradiction to the high level of trust that many men with AS said they had for their partners. It normally follows that if you totally trust someone you are able to talk to him or her about most things and are able to trust them with that information.

Many men said they felt threatened when asked direct questions by their partners and quite suspicious as to why she wanted to know and what she was going to do with the information if they supplied it. One man said that any personal questions from his wife felt like an intrusion. Another said that whatever he told his partner about himself was always used to criticize him at a later date.

Sensitivity to criticism appears to be very high amongst men with Asperger syndrome. Almost all the men I spoke to mentioned the feeling of being criticized by their partners. Criticism was also mentioned by all the NT partners, who felt every time they tried to talk about any problems they had, or if they tried to offer their partners advice or help them, they would instantly be accused of criticizing them.

To understand this it needs to be remembered that the AS person is often unaware that what he is doing or saying is wrong or hurtful; it might even be that it is the obvious absence of what he should be saying or doing that is causing the problem. One reason for this is the difficulty he has in being able to read her mind and understand her feelings. He cannot imagine, guess or work out what she is thinking and feeling and often why she is hurting. He cannot read the more subtle non-verbal signs she gives him and will not be aware that she is sad or hurt about something he has done or not done.

Second, his heightened sensitivity to criticism may be because what she is saying conflicts with his own perceived script about himself. It may be that he sees himself as someone who always tries to do his best, or who is caring. If what she is verbalizing disputes this or brings it into question, he will believe she is just being critical or attacking him. In the same way, if he discloses something about himself and then she argues with it or challenges what he is saying, he will interpret this as a betrayal on her part and also a direct criticism of himself. He wants verification and confirmation that his perception of himself is right. If she challenges this and he accepts it, he will have to revalidate his ideas and thoughts. He would need to change his perception of himself and this would be very difficult for him to do. So he hears her words as criticism rather than advice and in that way does not have to acknowledge what she is saying or act on her perceived criticism.

The only time I have seen AS men change their perception of themselves is when they have had a diagnosis and realized that what their partners were saying was true: there really was, for instance, a problem in communication – he did not always know what she wanted. For some adults with AS, finding that there is a reason for why they do not always get it right or why they cannot seem to make their partner happy comes as a complete revelation. The AS man is often relieved to know he is not to blame for what has been going wrong in the relationship and that he no longer needs to be so defensive or reactive when she highlights an area or task he has not done right. It is easy for the NT partner to forget that her partner may not know what it is he should say or how he should respond to a given situation. This may leave him feeling he is being accused of something he has no knowledge of, and so in most cases something he can do nothing about.

One couple came to see me and the wife said she could not live with her husband anymore. She went on to say she could not believe how anyone could be so cruel and heartless.

Apparently the couple had discussed the subject of sex the week before and this had led them to reminisce and reflect on the experiences they had shared together. They had talked about the very first time they had spent the night together. Her memory of this time was a very special one; they had courted for a long time before they had slept together. She disclosed to him how special it had been to her and asked him how it had been for him. He replied in all honesty that he had felt disappointed at the time. She was shocked by this and asked why he was disappointed. He said because he had expected her to have bigger breasts, and that he was surprised that one breast in particular was not as big as the other. She was absolutely devastated by this remark and her confidence and self-esteem took a severe knock.

We talked it through and he could not see why she was so angry at him when all he had done was be honest: she had asked him what he had thought and he had told her. It made no sense to him for her to ask him for his opinion and then get angry when he gave it. He asked me whether she had wanted him to lie to her. He had presented his partner with factual information in answer to what she had asked him because that was the easiest and most natural response for him to supply. He did not have the intuition to know that this was not the reply she wanted, and that telling her this would destroy her memories of what for her had been a very special and intimate time. He could only see the situation from his point of view and how it had affected him. His remark was painful and insensitive, but she asked for the truth and he gave her the truth. It was not his intention to cause her pain. It has been said that if you want the truth you should ask someone with Asperger syndrome.

The only way he could understand the pain he had caused was to relate it back to something that might have made *him* feel inadequate and inferior. This was the only way he could comprehend what effect his words had had on her. As a consequence of this incident he became very careful about what he said in the future. He adopted the word 'nice', so if he could not say it was nice he would disclose nothing at all.

Quite a few of the men said that they used to disclose things in the beginning but realized it was going to be used against them, so completely withdrew and offered no information that they felt might be abused. They were not wrong about this, because in most instances the information they had disclosed had caused a reaction from their partner. Unfortunately they had not made the connection about why it seemed to be used against them, or realized that this type of brutal honesty can be quite damaging to the other person.

Nearly all the NT women I spoke to said that initially they felt they could disclose most things to their partners. This had changed for them over a period of time. Although eighty per cent felt they could make disclosures to their partners, these were either not understood, or in some cases not even remembered by the AS partner. This had resulted in many of the women no longer disclosing their feelings and thoughts. One NT woman explained that although her husband would appear to listen he would not actually hear what she was saying; he was unable to comment on or empathize with what she said unless it was based on factual and logical information. She said it was as though he was deaf to her feelings in the same way that some people with impaired hearing cannot hear sounds at a certain pitch. He could not hear her feelings.

This 'feeling deafness' appears to be quite common amongst AS men. One woman described how as soon as the conversation with her husband progressed on to emotions and feelings her husband would say, ' Pardon, I cannot hear you, what did you say?' She would repeat what she had said. 'Look,' he would say, 'I really cannot hear a word you are saying, you are mumbling.' She would end up shouting, he would end up having an anger outburst. Eventually she gave up trying to communicate her feelings, which was very sad and frustrating for her. Another woman boasted that she could tell her husband anything at all, no matter how intimate and emotional the subject. 'That must be really good for you', I said, ' to be able to trust him that much.' 'Oh yes,' she laughed, 'he quite simply forgets everything I have said two minutes after I have said it!'

It does appear that AS men can have difficulty hearing and understanding their partner's disclosures about their feelings and emotions. One way to understand this is to imagine trying to listen to someone talking about a very specialist subject using very technical jargon. It would be very difficult to retain or remember what they had said if you did not understand the language and were not familiar with it. It appears to be very much like this for someone with Asperger syndrome. Unless the right words and terms are used, they will have difficulty listening and little chance of understanding.

One woman said that she had learned not to talk about anything she felt very deeply about because her husband would become depressed. It appears that AS men broadly divide into two camps: there are those who become angry and loud when they feel threatened, or if they think they are losing control; and those who completely withdraw and become distant or depressed. It is possible that both these reactions are forms of anger and frustration and for those who internalize the anger it can rapidly become depression. Depression is anger turned inwards; some people can express anger freely, others cannot. It is the same in cases of AS adults, except that Asperger syndrome seems to exaggerate the issue. This way anger can become explosive and withdrawal can cause deep depression. Whichever way the AS person deals with their anger it is their way of trying to gain control.

Control is as essential to adults with Asperger syndrome as air to breathe. Keeping control is the only way they feel they can survive in a complex world full of mixed emotions and inconsistent feelings, all of which are a complete mystery to them. They have to try and interpret a language they have no knowledge of; there are no guidebooks on the unspoken word. Given that seventy per cent of communication is unspoken, the remaining thirty per cent does not leave them with much information to get by on. No one is to blame for this, not the AS person or the person who is living with them. This is the message I give all my clients and it is important for the well-being of both that this is understood.

Improvement and change *can* be achieved in this problematic area. The AS person is often above average intelligence and can learn from a logical and practical route that there are right things to say and wrong things to say. He can learn to think before he speaks and to understand that some things are hurtful. The AS person who is committed to the relationship and wants to make things better can make a few improvements. It just takes time, motivation and an incentive on his part and a whole load of patience and understanding on hers.

Often some improvement can be made if he is able to understand on a practical level rather than an emotional level why he should do things differently. For example, one man never bought his wife flowers, he said he considered them a waste of money, they just died and went in the rubbish. He viewed buying flowers in a purely practical way. He did not see that yes, they did die and end up in the rubbish, but that was not the point, the point was that they gave pleasure to the person they were being given to.

'OK', I said to him, 'let's talk about the dinner you had last night, what did you eat?'

'Fish, broccoli and jacket potatoes,' he replied.

'That sounds nice, did you enjoy it?' I asked.

'Yes, it was salmon.'

'That's his favourite fish,' his wife intercepted, 'he likes it when I cook him salmon.'

'So your wife cooked your dinner for you last night,' I said. ' She went to the shop, bought your favourite fish, cooked it with broccoli and potatoes. You ate it up and it made you feel satisfied and looked after?'

'Yes,' he replied.

'Where is that dinner now?' I asked him.

'In the toilet, I suspect,' came his reluctant reply.

'So, maybe your wife could think feeding you was a waste of money and time, like you think buying her flowers is?'

'Ah, but this is different,' he replied quickly, 'she could think that, but it is not the same. I need to eat or I will starve. She does not need flowers to survive!'

'Your wife's emotional needs are just the same as your physical needs, they need to be fed and looked after too, and one way you can do this is to buy her flowers every now and then and show that you have thought about her and what makes her happy. She needs you to look after this side of her. I know it is difficult for you because you do not have the same needs, but you now know why that is and can understand that her needs are different to yours. You say you want to make her happy, well, this is one way you can do it. If you do this then maybe she will feel she has more emotional energy to look after your physical needs and cook your favourite fish.'

Guess who got a bouquet of flowers the next week, and on her birthday one month later? He just needed to see things from a perspective that he could understand and then he could be proactive about it.

Women with Asperger syndrome felt it was their partners who had problems in understanding the disclosures they made. One woman said she would spend ages trying to describe to him what she felt and within twenty-four hours he had completely forgotten what she had said. Many of the women, like the AS men, felt they could not trust their partner with information that might be used against them, but they did not appear to feel threatened by disclosure in the same way the AS men did. In fact most of the AS women had been very open and honest about themselves and tried very hard to explain to their partners how they felt. They expressed a lot of disappointment that their partners had failed to understand them, but not fear or regret about the repercussions or consequences of their disclosures.

Key points

- Few AS men feel able to disclose information about themselves to their partner.

- AS men say they feel threatened when asked direct questions by their partners.

- Some AS men believe that anything they disclose to their partner would be used to criticize them.

- AS men can sometimes reply to a disclosure or question that requires a sensitive reply with complete and sometimes brutal honesty.

- Both partners say that in the beginning of the relationship they were able to disclose information about themselves.

- The majority of NT women say that although they can make disclosures to their partners these disclosures were rarely understood by them.

- ○ 'Feeling deafness' is sometimes responsible for the AS partner's inability to hear and understand disclosures about feelings and emotions.
- ○ Maintaining control is vital to AS adults.
- ○ Most AS women are open and honest about themselves and do not feel threatened when making personal disclosures to their partners.

7

Communication

All the couples raised problems in communication as the subject that took precedence over all other difficulties within and outside their relationship. Breakdown in communication between a couple can cause misunderstandings, arguments, low self-esteem and frustration. Couples where one partner has Asperger syndrome often complain that they talk in two different languages, and in counselling, my role is often to act as interpreter between the two of them.

It is not surprising that communication is so high on the problem list, as it is one of the core traits caused by having Asperger syndrome. Difficulties in both verbal and non-verbal communication may be present, and it is likely the problems will be more extreme within the non-verbal area.

For certain AS men, verbal communication is less of a problem, and they are quite good communicators, able to talk endlessly about their work or interests. When talking about their favourite topics they can be very interesting and entertaining. Some men with Asperger syndrome can use words in a most articulate and expressive way; their knowledge of language allows them to use uncommon words in a very expert manner. This can certainly give the impression of an excellent communicator and a few of the NT women said their first impression of their partner was that he was talkative, witty and expressive. He appeared interesting and could easily demand the respect of others and give the impression of power and intelligence.

Other AS men are experts at accents and languages and can imitate accents, which makes them very entertaining when telling jokes or reporting what someone from another area had said. In certain cases, picking up another language comes easily, and when in a foreign country an AS person could soon be talking with such perfect fluency that others may have believed that they were talking in their native tongue. Many people with Asperger syndrome, especially women, are brilliant actors and excellent at mimicking. Mimicry is often displayed in autistic children and it may be that the ability to imitate is an extension of this autistic trait. Mimicry can be a source of frustration for the NT partner though, who can find it very belittling to have someone appearing to mock them. One woman explained how frustrating it was that her partner constantly copied her laugh. She had an unusual laugh and felt that her partner had mimicked her to the point where she stopped laughing. She felt he had stolen a piece of her.

Not all AS men are talkative though; others can appear to be quite shy, quiet and uncommunicative, talking very little. Most would interpret this lack of communication as being introverted or not having the confidence to interact with others. I discovered, when talking to one couple, this is not always the reason. They came to see me with various issues but one of the major problems was that of communication, or lack of it. The woman explained that he would not talk to her and could remain silent for days. She felt she was slowly going mad with the loneliness and frustration this was causing her. Her partner listened while she spoke, offering no response or feedback at all. This gave the initial impression that he was indeed a very quiet and introverted man with extreme problems in communicating.

I turned the conversation round to him and found he responded quite easily and answered my questions. This, though, was all he did, answering with as few words as possible. Then I asked him about his work. He told me he was a computer scientist and at this point he came alive and talked about his latest discovery and how keen he was to try it out and what he thought it would achieve. I had some knowledge of the subject in question, so was able to hold my own, offer him some interesting comments and ask some relevant questions. This encouraged him further and it became more and more apparent that this man had no problems with the actual process of communication and interaction when it was a subject he was interested in. He did not at any time involve his wife in our conversation and when I tried to bring her in he totally ignored what she had to say.

I asked him why he did not communicate with his wife, to which he replied that there was no point. I asked if he would explain to me what he meant by that.

'I would rather not talk at all,' he coldly replied.

His wife looked very hurt and said that was very cruel of him, as he knew how much she wanted him to talk to her. He repeated that he would rather not talk than have to converse with her. I asked him if he could tell us why he felt like this towards his wife, to which he replied that she was not intelligent enough for him to talk to. At this his wife was even more hurt; she was by no means an unintelligent woman!

I asked him to explain further and he said she could not understand the subjects he wished to talk about and found some of her responses an insult to the nature of the work he was involved in. I asked why he could not enter into dialogue with her on a subject she was conversant with.

'Why should I?' he said, 'I have no interest in cooking, children or her friends.'

This man was only seeing things from his perspective and, although he said he was not aiming to be cruel or unkind to his wife, this was without doubt the way his message came across. He was unable to understand why she was so upset because, after all, he had only been honest. In his opinion their interests were so different that he could not enter or discuss her world, it was trivial and unimportant to him. He did not expect her to discuss his subject with him because he felt she could not offer anything beyond what he already knew. He did not particularly want to talk about anything else and so did not.

In addition to wanting only to talk about subjects that interested them, some AS men do not talk because they are afraid that they will say the wrong thing, especially if the subject matter approaches the delicate topic of feelings or emotions. AS men deal with this fear in two different ways. Some get very angry and frustrated and use this in order to silence their partner. Others seem to shut down, a visible process that I have seen many times while talking to couples. He will become aware that the conversation and his partner are getting emotional and he is being required to talk about feelings and emotions. He starts to show signs of feeling uncomfortable by taking longer to reply, using many 'umms' and 'ahhs', choosing his words very carefully, each sentence being thought out and analysed. He may start to fidget in his chair or wring his hands together. At this point he will either get angry or stop speaking altogether.

I have talked earlier about the differences in brain processing between AS people and NT people. When the AS person is asked a question or presented with a problem that involves reading someone else's feelings or putting him or herself in someone else's mind, he is unable to use the part of the brain designed for this purpose and used by NT people. He instead uses the area of the brain that is used for logical and practical problem solving. The AS person when sorting out an issue that requires insightful thought can only produce an answer by using a logical and practical route. His attempts to give an appropriate answer by using a different prob-lem-solving process are very difficult. He has already learned by trial and error that the answer that comes automatically to him is rarely the one that will be greeted with a happy or welcoming response. The AS man discovers over time that his reply seems to provoke anger, make his partner upset or very reactive and, as that is not his intention, he interprets this reaction as a direct criticism and attack on him.

This is why so many conversations between couples break down when one partner has Asperger syndrome. Often the NT partner is left feeling that it is impossible to get him to understand or grasp the point she is trying to make and this is the cause of much frustration for both of them. The whole point of the interaction gets totally lost in a sea of confusion and drowning emotions. Many women talk about how they and their partner seem to talk in different languages and have no comprehension of what the other is saying or meaning.

Often I encounter a very frustrated and almost desperate woman saying:

Why is it he cannot talk about emotions?

Why does he never get the point?

Why does something so straightforward end up so complicated?

Why does he never hear what I am saying?

Why does he always accuse me of criticizing him, when I am trying to help him?

Why does he hurt the children and me with his insensitive comments?

The list goes on and on and it is interesting that so many women are saying exactly the same things about their situation and partner. It really is a huge issue for the NT partner. But what about the partner with Asperger syndrome, how big a problem is communication for them?

Key points

- Problems in communication take precedence over all other difficulties in the relationship with an AS partner.
- The level of verbal communication in AS men varies considerably.
- Some adults with AS are excellent at mimicking and although this can be amusing, it can be perceived as hurtful by the partner.
- It has been known for an AS man not to communicate with his partner unless absolutely necessary.
- AS men can find talking about their feelings very difficult.
- The AS and the NT partners are often left feeling they talk in different languages.
- Most NT partners seem to use the same terminology to describe their feelings when trying to communicate with their partner.

8

The Asperger Syndrome Side
of Communication

The question 'How much of a problem do you think communication is in your relationship?' evoked a far more detailed and lengthy response than any other question I asked. Without exception, all the AS men answered that this area was one of the most problematic in their relationships and most recognized that this was directly attributable to them. However, in addition, some thought that a large proportion of the problem was related to their partner's reaction to what they said or the manner in which it was said. Others felt that it was their partner who completely misinterpreted what they had said. Many of the AS men voiced that they felt victimized and highly criticized in this area. Others complained that their partners had tried to change them but all felt they had absolutely no idea as to what they were supposed to be changing to.

A significant number of AS men felt they were very misunderstood by their partners. One man reported that his wife constantly accused him of responding in the wrong tone of voice. He said she often took offence at something he had said, when his intention was quite the opposite.

'It is the way I talk. I do not know how to talk in another way, I do not have another voice!' he argued. 'She wants me to change… I cannot change my voice.'

I acknowledged that this must be very frustrating for him.

'It is!' he exclaimed, 'and then she wants me to say sorry, she expects me to apologize for something I have not done. I won't and the argument goes on and on. I will not apologize for something I did not do; she does not apologize for taking offence when none was meant!'

This man felt strongly that his partner was totally unjustified in her expectations of him to make changes to something he was unaware of and did not feel he had any control over.

Three men reported that their partners had told them that they were boring and never thought of interesting subjects on which to converse. Most knew exactly how they could change this, because their partners had told them. They reported having been told to read about different subjects, read the papers, join a college class or take up a new interest. Despite knowing what they could do to facilitate change, hardly any of the men converted the theory into practice. It can be very difficult for a person with Asperger syndrome to focus his mind on a subject in which he has little or no interest. This is due to the narrow and fixed area of interest often displayed in those with Asperger syndrome; although they may be experts on their chosen field or subject, they may show no interest whatsoever in anything else.

This disinterest in other subjects can cause problems in socializing as AS people seldom have the discretion to hide this. When in the company of others, they can actually be observed switching off their attention when the subject being mooted is on a subject that is of no interest to them. Furthermore, it has been observed that in some cases they will actually walk away, leaving the other person standing there talking to themselves. This can also be seen in relationships when the partner brings up a topic that is of no interest to the AS man. He may not listen, he may interrupt and change the topic of conversation or, if all of this fails, he may just walk away.

Interrupting was a point raised by two of the men who complained that they were constantly reprimanded by their partners for interrupting them or others whilst in conversation. There are often occasions when we find ourselves in a dialogue with someone who is conversing on a subject that is of little or no interest to us. Most people when placed in this position will be polite and tolerate the situation, especially when it is their partner and they are both in the company of others. However, some people with Asperger syndrome may constantly interrupt or talk over their partners and this will eventually cause a reaction, probably one of anger. It was the consensus of opinion that this reaction is totally unjustified. One man said he wanted to add a very valuable and relevant point to a conversation and if it was not voiced immediately, the conversation subject would change and those in discussion would miss his contribution.

Again, this indicates the AS person's difficulty in seeing things from the other people's perspective. Maybe there was no need for them to know what he had to say, especially as they would never have known he was going to say it in the first place. It is as though, because he knows what they may miss if his contribution is not voiced, he assumes they too will miss it. The introspective thinking that is often part of Asperger syndrome causes this. Once again the person with AS truly believes he has every one else's best interests at heart.

The same logic is applied when an AS person moves onto his favourite topic or special interest. I have often seen a woman almost panic when she hears someone ask her partner about his favourite subject, and desperately try to intervene and redirect the conversation onto any other topic. This rarely succeeds as he probably has not even heard or been aware of what she was trying to do.

A few of the AS men complained that their partners accused them of not listening, and claimed that their partners will say that they have told them things that they are sure they haven't. Selective hearing is an issue raised by the majority, if not all, of the NT women I spoke to, and seems to be the catalyst for many of the disagreements that evolve between the couples. There is a high level of probability that the NT women have given their AS partners the information, but the AS person does not have any memory of what she has said. The reason is that the information probably never reached long-term memory.

In order to retain information, the message received has to be encoded and reach our long-term memory stores. Long-term memory is like a library in our brain that sorts and categorizes our memories in our memory banks, ready to be retrieved when required. Before information can reach long-term memory, it has to pass through short-term memory. Short-term memory is very different from long-term memory and lasts only a matter of seconds. If the message is not heard and encoded it will not reach its destination in the long-term memory stores and will therefore not be retained for retrieval later.

There are many reasons why messages do not reach long-term memory and one of them is distraction. Distraction can make it very difficult to concentrate and, according to Allan and Barbara Pease in their book *Why Men Don't Listen & Women Can't Read Maps*, men are particularly susceptible to being distracted and find it very difficult to do more than one task at a time. This particular problem seems to be exacerbated by having Asperger syndrome and makes it very difficult for an AS man to concentrate on what is being said if there are any distractions at the time.

As an example, one woman told her husband that she had arranged for them both to pick up her mother that evening. It was her mum's birthday and they were taking her out for a meal. She finished by asking him if he could come home from work early because she needed a hand getting the kids sorted for bed before the babysitter came round. She told him this whilst the family were eating breakfast. He was sitting in front of her at the time and appeared to be listening and absorbing what she was saying. That night, however, he did not come home early, and when he did eventually arrive, he said he had no idea what she was talking about and accused her of not telling him. This infuriated her as she knew that she had told him and the thought occurred to her that this was his ploy to avoid going to see his mother-in-law. The evening was ruined for everyone, she was angry at his accusations that she was trying to get at him, he was frustrated that she still insisted that she had told him things that he clearly thought that she had not, and to cap it all, poor Mum did not get to go out.

So why didn't he hear the information his wife had given him? First, the radio was on while she was talking to him, second the kids were at the table and he had noticed the youngest was dribbling her drink down her clean dress. Finally he had remembered he needed to phone someone before they left for work as he needed them to bring in a new computer program that he wanted to try out at work that day. This was too much distraction and the consequence was sensory overload – the information from his wife never got through the barriers. Although he was hearing the words his wife had said, the message had never made it to long-term memory, therefore there was no memory of what she had said for him to retrieve.

In the counselling room I frequently ask the AS person to repeat back to me what I have said and then to clarify that they understand what I have said in the way I meant it. This constant checking out can feel tedious and time consuming for the NT partner, but it really is vital if she does not want to encounter situations similar to the one I have just described.

Another area of communication where forty per cent of AS men said they felt very criticized was their partners' accusations that they refused to discuss deep and meaningful topics. Although the AS men were aware that they did not discuss such subjects with their partners, they felt they were insinuating that they did not have any feelings or emotions. Topics involving feelings and emotions, and understanding these, were usually very difficult or impossible for the AS men to discuss. This is not because they do not have feelings, they have feelings just like anyone else, but the feelings they have are only ever personal to them; they are not able to empathize with someone else's feelings. This may result in the AS person making assumptions about the way someone feels, but based on his own feeling at the time or how he remembers feeling in a similar situation in the past. There is a lack of awareness that someone else may feel quite differently, even if the contributing factors are similar.

Another point raised by some of the men in my research was that their partners expected them to know how they would feel in a situation that has not yet occurred. Let me elucidate. One couple had made an agreement at an early stage of their relationship that they would be completely open and honest with each other about money and finances. They ran a small business together and she dealt with most of the financial aspects of the business and home. She trusted her partner completely and it never occurred to her that he would betray this trust. It came as a great shock therefore when she discovered that he had run up debts buying goods over the Internet. She challenged him about it and he said he had not realized he had overspent and he would make sure the debt was settled. She felt betrayed by his silence and let down after they had made such a firm agreement between them regarding finances. He was absolutely shocked that she was so upset by his actions. She accused him of being thoughtless and not considering her feelings. He still maintained that he had no idea that she would react so badly to his overspending.

Both partners were justified in their thinking. She was quite correct that he had not thought about what she would feel when she discovered his debts. This was not because he was being thoughtless or uncaring, but because he was unable to imagine how she would react emotionally to a situation that has not occurred previously between them. Even though she had told him how important it was for him to be open and honest with her about his spending, this was not enough for him to be able to predict her emotional response. This was a new situation and he had no preformatted schema to enable him to know logically how she would react. This is another difficulty in relationships that appears to be a direct consequence of having Asperger syndrome.

Lack of empathy for his partner's feelings can make the AS man appear very insensitive and uncaring and it is likely that he has been informed of this by his partner many times. The result is that for fear of saying the wrong thing he will do anything to avoid having to express his feelings or talk about emotions. One man said he would become angry with his wife if she brought up the subject of feelings or emotions. He said he took this action so she would not talk about them because it made him feel inadequate when he could not do what she wanted. Anger directed at her was his way of maintaining control of the conversation and of his wife. He said he needed to be in control and was totally unaware of the damage this was doing to her and to their relationship. It was only with many weeks of counselling that he came to develop different strategies in which to cope with the way emotional conversations made him feel. Both he and his wife had to change the way they did things in the relationship in order for this to work, and they both had to want it to work. Commitment to the relationship and wanting it to work, plus an awareness of Asperger syndrome and its implications, are imperative if any change or improvement to the couple's relationship is to be achieved. Without this commitment and desire, nothing will change.

Choice of words also plays a relevant role in whether communication flows smoothly. One man expressed his annoyance when his wife asked him if he could put a mirror up on the bathroom wall for her. 'She obviously thinks I am incapable of doing anything,' he argued. His pride was very wounded and his wife could not understand what she had done to upset him so much. I asked him why he was so defensive about her request. 'Well, she obviously thinks I am not capable of putting a mirror up on the wall.' His wife argued that that was not what she meant. It transpired that the whole misunderstanding had been caused because she had used the word 'could' and not 'would'. He felt that 'could' inferred that she had questioned his ability and that the word 'would' meant she was asking him to actually undertake the task. Something as simple as one word or, in this case, one letter can make a difference to what the person with AS hears and interprets.

Forty per cent of AS men said they felt very inadequate in the way they communicated with their partners and had found different ways of dealing with the way these inadequacies made them feel. Some blamed their wives; others blamed themselves. Very few blamed Asperger syndrome. One of the reasons for this was the lack of awareness shown by many AS men as to how AS affects communication. If there is no understanding of the syndrome, then the blame will be either taken personally or projected onto the partner.

One man said that he and his wife did not talk to each other. I asked him why this was the case and he told me that she was constantly trying to get him to understand what she was feeling and to understand the reasons that their problems developed in the first place. I said that maybe this was her way of trying to improve things and help him see things from her perspective. He replied that that was not the case and she was doing it to get at him and make him feel inadequate. I asked why he thought this and he replied that she was asking him to do something that was not possible and expected him to be able to do it. 'What was she asking you to do?' I asked. He answered that she was constantly asking why he could not try and see how she feels for a change. 'How can anyone see how someone feels?' he asked me. 'It cannot be done, it cannot be done, and she is just trying to put me down. So to negate the problem, I do not talk to her.' Because the AS person may interpret messages in the literal sense, words need to be chosen carefully. This man was rightly questioning how one could *see* a feeling.

Taking things literally is a feature of Asperger syndrome and can cause many misunderstandings. This is just one more area in communication that is so problematic for couples.

AS women also had problems with communication. The reasons they gave though, were very different from those given by the AS men. One woman said that the problems they had in communication were caused by her partner's inability to communicate on an effective level. She also added that she did not believe that he had any problems with the way she communicated. This opinion was shared by the majority of the AS women I contacted. Some said their partners did not listen to them or remember what they had said and others recounted that when their partner did communicate, he said the wrong thing or came out with a very hurtful or insensitive remark.

None of the AS women suggested that their partner had blamed or accused them of being unable to talk about feelings or emotions. This was very different from the reports by the AS men and is conceivably because the women in this study were in relationships with men who also had Asperger syndrome. These men's demands were probably quite different from those expressed by NT women.

This research shows first that communication is a major problem, even when both partners have Asperger syndrome, and second that it appears that all the women in relationships with AS men, whether they have AS or not, say that they are not being heard or responded to.

One of the reasons that messages are so often misunderstood or not heard is difficulty in reading the non-verbal signals that form a vital part in successful communication. The ability to receive and transmit non-verbal signals comes naturally to the NT person. It does not, however, come naturally to a person with AS. The problems this causes for couples can be catastrophic.

Key points

- ○ AS men feel communication is one of the most problematic areas in their relationships.
- ○ Many AS men feel criticized and victimized in this area.
- ○ Some AS men say their partners accuse them of being boring and not talking about interesting subjects.
- ○ Some AS men complain that their partners accuse them of interrupting.
- ○ Many AS men complain that their partners accuse them of not listening.

- ○ Messages given by the NT partner may never reach the long-term memory of the AS men.

- ○ Many AS men feel their partner expect them to discuss feelings and to be able to predict her reaction in a situation before it occurred.

- ○ Many AS men feel inadequate in the way they communicate.

- ○ On occasions the AS man will interpret messages literally, not grasping the real meaning.

- ○ AS women say the problems they have in communication are caused by their AS partners.

9

Non-verbal Communication –
The Unspoken Word

The bulk of communication is non-verbal, and is conveyed in many ways including facial expression, body language, tone of voice, emphasis on certain words and eye contact. It relies heavily on being able to interpret and understand the meaning behind the words. For instance, the words 'I am so fed up' can be said in different ways and may mean that the person saying them is very angry or very depressed. It depends on the tone of voice, which words are emphasized and the body language that goes with it, besides reading the message in context.

The ability to read non-verbal communication and give out accurate signals to others is often severely affected in Asperger syndrome. This can cause problems in relationships as often, unless a message is spoken, the AS person will not be able to figure out what is meant. Hence the man who constantly asks his wife if she is OK, because he cannot read it in her body language and facial expression.

It is often the more subtle expressions that are confused rather than the explicit ones; a smile is a smile and tears are tears, and the person with AS has few problems figuring out what they mean, unless they are used in sarcasm or to deceive. Where NT people have a natural ability to read non-verbal body language, for people with AS it can make communication and social interaction a nightmare. This is why it was initially surprising that sixty per cent of the men and women with Asperger syndrome were unaware that they had a problem in this particular area of communication.

This conflicted strongly with what their partners were saying about the problems they had reading and being read by their AS partner.

This lack of awareness in AS men, however, does make sense if one thinks about non-verbal communication and how it is so taken for granted by NT people. Try to imagine that, after many years, you discover that other people on this planet could read what someone was thinking if that person wanted them to, and you were one of the few people who could not do this. You would have grown up in the world without this knowledge because all those around would have presumed you had the ability, which was natural and automatic. It would not have occurred to them that you could not do this and it was therefore never questioned by them and, of course, you never said anything. Because you did not know this ability existed, you just struggled to understand people according to what they said and the non-verbal language they used, and when they got upset because you had not read their internal thoughts, you could not understand what you had done wrong. How could you have known what they meant? Why had they not communicated to you what they meant? Your partner accuses you of giving out the wrong signals and not sending the right thought patterns. This is simply because you do not have and have never had this ability. You can work things out up to a point, but could never reach the level that other people can, because this ability to read minds does not exist in you.

If you can imagine what this would feel like, you will be able to grasp what it is like for people with Asperger syndrome and just how confusing the whole process of communication is for them. Many are aware that they have a problem in verbal communication and because, like their partner, they can speak, listen and respond, they have some control over this. However, as they cannot read the more subtle non-verbal signals that NT people interpret quite naturally, they are not aware that someone else is able to do this until it is explained and pointed out.

One man said that he was not aware he had a problem in this area and if he did, it existed at a very low level. His wife looked at him in total frustration and disbelief.

'How can you say that?' she responded. 'You have not got a clue what I am trying to tell you half the time.'

He argued that of course he couldn't know what she was trying to tell him if she did not say it and went out of her way to hide it from him.

'Oh no, I do not!' she said, 'Everyone says what an expressive person I am, everyone else understands how I feel, it is just you, you do not care how I feel.'

He became very defensive and said she was attacking him again.

We spent a lot of time on the issue of non-verbal communication, and eventually things did improve. She learned to say what she was thinking and he learned to read the more basic signs; realizing that if she was sad or annoyed it was not always because of something he had done. He knew this because she had agreed to tell him if it was.

This direct form of communication comes as a tremendous relief to many partners with Asperger syndrome. It takes all of the guesswork out of communication. If he knows that she will say to him directly if there is something she wants him to do, rather than expect him to guess by reading her mind, he no longer has to worry that he may be missing a vital piece of information. It is very difficult for the NT partner to change her whole way of communicating and takes tremendous effort and patience on her part. It will not seem natural to spell out her every thought.

Most adults in relationships want to feel understood naturally by their partners; for many of us it is a sign of intimacy and love. We hear others making comments like, 'He knows me so well,' 'He just understands when I am down, I do not have to tell him,' or 'He knows me inside out, he loves me so much.' And we want to hear comments like these from our partners. This is not unusual or unrealistic, it is a basic human requirement longed for by many women in a relationship. Many NT women have told me of their desire to feel understood and valued for who they are and the qualities they have to offer. Most women are highly intuitive and perceive this as a quality they have to offer to their partner and family. They know when the kids are down or sick, they know when their partner is worried about an issue or decision he has to make, they can sense an atmosphere or know when a comment has been interpreted the wrong way. They seek the same response from their partner; they want him to understand and read their feelings, and often feel let down when he does not.

This need for the AS man to read her feelings will not be fulfilled, it will not happen because it cannot happen. It is not purposely withheld, it is an ability that the AS person does not have. It is only when she accepts this that she looks for his expressions of love and care in another direction. In other words she does not measure his love according to how he reads her feelings and makes her feel understood. He quite simply does not have this ability and it is not an indication that he does not love her. He is capable of finding other ways to show his love, more practical and active ways.

Other ways that women felt their AS partners struggled with non-verbal language was in the lack of expression in their voices and faces. This was mentioned by ten per cent of the AS men who said their partners complained about their lack of expressive communication. One man said he was just a bore and apologized to his wife for this. The most exciting and exhilarating topic can become completely boring if told in an emotionless and inexpressive way.

If Asperger syndrome is recognized in childhood, elocution lessons or speech therapy may be offered, as both can improve voice tone and expression. Unfortunately for the newly discovered AS adult this support is not always available or successful. How someone talks and expresses him or herself can be just as important when creating a first impression as how he or she looks or dresses. This can be especially important in job interviews and in the social field. It can make the difference in getting a job and forming new relationships. I have encountered many very capable, qualified and hardworking men with AS who apply for a job well within their competencies, only to be let down at the interview stage. This can happen time and time again: their difficulties in communication and expressing themselves give the interviewer a false impression and they do not get the job. This is for some a sad but very real consequence of having Asperger syndrome and it can seriously damage self-esteem and feelings of being valued.

Next we look at how the AS adult survives socially, given the difficulties that having AS can create for him. We also look at how his partner survives with him and the problems there can be within the couple relationship.

Key points

- The ability to read non-verbal communication and give out accurate signals to others is often severely affected in Asperger syndrome.

- Many AS men and women are unaware that they have a problem in the area of non-verbal communication.

- The NT partner has to learn to say exactly what they mean to the AS person in order to be understood.

- The NT partner's need for the AS partner to read her feelings will not be fulfilled.

- Some AS men say their partners complain that they are expressionless in their communication.

- Difficulties in communication and expression can give a negative and false impression of the AS adult's abilities.

10

Social Scenes

Socializing, like communication, is one of the core areas affected by Asperger syndrome. For many couples it is only the sense of humour of the NT partner that gets them through sensitive situations.

One woman talked about how she had arranged with her family and friends to go out for a meal for her daughter's sixteenth birthday. She had booked a table in the non-smoking area of the restaurant, as she knew her husband had a great aversion to cigarette smoke. On the way to the restaurant her husband wanted to fill the car up with fuel. He only liked one particular garage, because they supplied plastic gloves for customers to wear while putting the petrol in. They all had to detour in completely the wrong direction to this particular garage, they were already running late and the atmosphere in the car was becoming tense to say the least. When they arrived late and the table she had booked had been taken, they were offered another table in a smoking area. It was too late to risk going anywhere else so she took her husband aside and asked him quietly to just this once tolerate it for his daughter's sake.

It was unfortunate that they sat next to a table of smokers. She could feel the tension building up in her partner, who had been waving his hands about and making it obvious that the smoke was bothering him. Suddenly he stood up and went over to the smokers' table. He informed them that he and his family wished to eat without getting lung cancer and would they mind either putting out their cigarettes or opening the window behind them. You could have cut the atmosphere with a knife: their daughter ran out of the restaurant, embarrassed that her dad could cause such a scene in front of her two classmates. The poor wife did not know what to do for the best. She could see a scene developing between the people on the other table and her husband, she wanted to apologize to her friends, the manager had been called and was making his way over to their table. In the end she did the only thing a mother could do, seek out and comfort her daughter who was crying her eyes out in the ladies toilet.

Time has passed since this incident and she can now laugh at the situation, but it is unlikely that their daughter will ever forget it.

When I asked AS adults whether they thought they had a problem with socializing the replies were very varied: twenty per cent said they had no problems at all, while forty per cent chose to not socialize. Stating that they had no problems socializing may seem strange considering that social interaction is a core area affected by AS, and adds further testimony to the complex and varied nature of Asperger syndrome.

It seems that as well as being affected to a greater or lesser degree on the autistic spectrum, individuals are also affected at different levels within the core disabilities caused by the syndrome. It appears possible that some adults with Asperger syndrome may have full ability in communication but little insight and empathy. Others may be relatively comfortable in the company of others but not need to communicate. There does seem to be a lot of variance in the level of effect these three core areas in Asperger syndrome have on an individual. Each of the three areas will be affected to some degree, but sometimes it can appear that a particular area is Asperger free. This can be sometimes misleading as only with closer examination do the difficulties make themselves apparent.

For instance, I may talk to one individual who appears quite capable of holding an interesting and easily flowing conversation. We may talk for a while about his job, his relationship with his family and so on. Very little about the way he presents himself and communicates would indicate that he had Asperger syndrome. However, I may then ask him to tell me about his wife and what it is about her he loves. Silence! His face may pull an expression that does not fit; he may tighten his lips or raise his eyes upwards while he searches his memory for a suitable answer. 'Well, she seemed nice when I met her and I liked her hair.' This reply does not really answer either question, but without rehearsal it was the quickest reply he could think of. So although this man was good at verbalizing himself, it was based on whether he controlled the conversation and what it was about, which is why many AS adults will try to divert the conversation onto what they want to talk about and feel comfortable with.

How at ease and comfortable AS men felt in a situation was stated as crucial to whether they socialized or tolerated a particular situation. There are times when most of us feel uncomfortable in a particular social situation. We walk into a room and instantly start to read what is going on around us. We may head for the food table because that gives us something to do, we may look for someone we know or we may spot the person with the welcoming smile. Reading social situations is very difficult for people with Asperger syndrome and they do not always get it right. Due to the difficulty they have reading other peoples' reactions they may not always realize when they get it wrong or offend someone, and because of this they may have the false belief that they are doing OK. Unless they are aware of AS and listen to what their partner or others are telling them they may conclude that they do not have any problems socializing with other people. It is often their partner or family that carries the embarrassment and has to cope with the problems the AS man can unknowingly and innocently cause.

One man told me that he had no problems socializing, but his wife disagreed and went on to say that he did not like smoking or drinking so would not go to dances, pubs or hotels, and only liked specific foods so most restaurants were ruled out. Trying to find a non-smoking eating place that served the food he enjoyed was very nearly impossible. This meant that if she wanted to go anywhere she had to go alone – if there was any family celebration or special gathering he would not go. This was difficult because she wanted him to be with her and found it embarrassing to keep making excuses for his absence. So when he said he did not have any problems socializing, this was a very honest and accurate answer from his perspective, because he did not go anywhere to socialize, and when he said he liked most people and did not mind talking to them he was also being honest. It was some of their habits and the food that he did not like. This man was seeing things only from his perspective and felt strongly that his wife was telling lies about him to make him look bad.

However, many men were acutely aware of what their partners said about them with respect to their socializing abilities and I was given many details of what they had been accused of. Fifteen per cent of the AS men stated that their partners had accused them of being rude to other people or interrupting conversations, and all argued strongly that this was never their intention or meant to cause offence. Some said this had caused major problems in their relationship.

One NT woman said she had bought a slinky black dress for a dinner dance they were going to. She asked her husband if her bottom looked big in it. He asked her to turn round, and told her, actually yes, it does look very big! This was not the reply she had wanted! She thanked him for his answer (sarcastically) and he said that was OK, not recognising the hurt or sarcasm in her voice. She felt very injured and put down by his response and he was completely unaware of the pain he had caused her. We talked about this together, and when he did understand that he had said the wrong thing, he asked a very thought-provoking question.

'Maybe, then, you can tell me why people ask these questions in the first place if they do not want an honest reply, and if the person is not going to give an honest reply because that is the social rule how can anyone ever gain from the communication? How is my wife ever to know whether her bottom looks big or not? I am totally confused,' he said, waiting for my reply.

Observations like this certainly can make us question whose way of thinking is the more normal. I have to agree that many of our social rules are based on play-acting and saying what the other person wants. Has society become so self-centred and dishonest? We call them white lies, but to the AS mind, a lie is a lie whatever colour we try and convince them it is. A white lie does not exist in the Asperger syndrome vocabulary and, although it can seem quite hard to hear the truth at times, it can be refreshing to know that what you have heard is a true opinion.

AS adults do, though, learn in relationships that a truthful opinion is not always the right one to give and that they are expected to skirt the direct approach. This can be very difficult for them as most do not make very good natural liars. They do not have the same ability that some NT adults may have to lie and 'sweet talk'. One reason is that it is harder for the AS adult to disguise the lie and make it look like the truth. In order to be a good liar one has to match words with vocal tone, facial expressions and body language. When the AS adult attempts to lie, it can be so obvious that the partner may misread it as sarcasm. Either way, the AS adult may appear to be rude, when in fact this was probably not the intention.

This is not to say that the AS adult never intends to be rude, he is just as capable as anyone else of being critical and derogatory in order to manipulate or gain control of a situation. For example: one man did not like his wife going out with her friend; he felt she was a bad influence on his wife. When his wife was getting ready to go out he came into the bedroom, looked at her, and told her he was disappointed that she had started to dress down, and that he would have expected a higher standard from her than that! She was shocked and taken aback by this remark and reacted quite strongly to it. This resulted in a row and both sides said some very hurtful things.

The couple discussed this with me and I asked her what she was wearing. She said she was wearing just a skirt and top. I asked if she could describe the outfit to me. The outfit it turned out was a low-cut top and a short skirt. I asked her husband what he had thought about the clothes she was wearing and he said she had worn clothes like that when he had met her and he had been attracted to her, therefore it was an outfit to make her attractive to men. As she was not going out with him, he had assumed it could only be to attract other men. 'All I get are the tatty jeans and baggy sweaters,' he said, in a very sullen and victimized voice.

It had not occurred to him to tell his wife how he really felt, which was that she looked very attractive and he felt very threatened and insecure. He had presumed she would automatically know how he felt. In his mind she was aware of the reason she had dressed up and was therefore aware of what she was doing, so she would automatically know how her actions made him feel.

Due to the difficulty in empathizing with and being able to read and understand the mind of the NT partner, this breakdown in interaction happens all too often. The AS adult can only see things from his point of view, from his perception; he may also believe he can understand his partner's perception too. Unfortunately, this is likely to be based directly on a personal experience he has had and on the false belief that she knows what he is thinking.

Misunderstandings in social interaction can be frequent and, every now and then, his actions or words may upset someone and he may not be aware of what he has said or done unless the offended person points it out to him. If this is explained in a way he can understand and fits in with the personal script he has given for himself, he may realize his error. If it is not explained well and he cannot accept that, even unintentionally, he has been rude, then he will have great problems seeing that what he did may have offended the other person. He will see that it is the other person who has the problem, not him.

One woman said her husband was quite good at talking to people, but because he could be quite rude, he often upset people and consequently, many would not talk to him. I asked her to explain exactly what he did, and she related what had happened the previous weekend. They had gone to a work dinner party at her friend's house. She told him that her friend was quite into biking, and he had presumed from this that she had meant cycling so he was very shocked to discover it was motorbikes not cycling bikes! He struggled very hard with this concept, bikes were not something he liked and he could certainly not accept that they could be a female pastime.

When her friend announced that she had bought a new motorbike, his face said it all, his eyebrows went up, his mouth made an exaggerated grimace. His expression was so rude that he did not need to say anything. Her friend tactfully ignored his expression and continued to tell her work colleagues that she had found a new boyfriend who also liked bikes. Her husband looked at her friend and said, 'What do you need a boyfriend for when you have that throbbing piece of metal between your legs?' The whole group went totally silent; the silence seemed to last forever. Her friend fortunately had a good sense of humour, laughed it off and moved the subject on quickly to another topic.

When his wife questioned him later, he said he had been trying to make a joke and could not understand why anyone in their right mind would want to ride a motorbike when they could drive in the comfort of a car! He had no intention of being rude and was completely unaware he had offended anyone. He was, though, aware that he had felt uncomfortable and said he had often felt uncomfortable in social situations but did not know why.

Misreading the signals can cause a lot of problems when socializing and this works both ways. The AS adult may pick up that there is a problem because they feel uncomfortable, but they may not always be aware of the reason or that they may have played a part in it. It is very difficult for an AS adult to read the more subtle signs of non-verbal language, they will pick up on the obvious if someone cries or smiles or frowns, and try to find an association with the facial expression; perhaps it is because she is watching a sad film or has just received a card from one of the children. If, on the other hand, he sees her staring at him in a social situation desperately trying to tell him without words to shut up, he will not have a clue what she is trying to tell him and probably ask her out loud why she is pulling faces at him. This will only add to the embarrassment she is already feeling.

Being aware that something you have done or said has been out of place and noticed by others causes most people embarrassment. Embarrassment acts as a deterrent that often keeps us in our place, makes us aware of our actions and, if we get it wrong, can make us feel very conscious of ourselves. Many people with AS do not appear to experience feelings of embarrassment; this may be due to the inability to read other people's thoughts. The AS person will often be totally unaware that he has said or done anything untoward and consequently rarely feel or show embarrassment. If an NT person can imagine what it is like to not know or feel embarrassment then she will understand how one would not be aware of being offensive or upsetting to someone else. Hence NT women can find themselves in some very difficult social situations, with their AS partners totally unaware of the problems they may have caused. This can lead to other people avoiding the couple and unfortunately increase the loneliness and isolation that the NT adult feels.

An AS man told me how, sometimes, he would meet someone and take an instant dislike to them and find it almost impossible not to let it show. When I asked him how he dealt with this, he said he would often ignore them. One of the reasons he gave for disliking people was because of the way they talked or their tone of voice. Some AS men have expressed annoyance at the voices of some people they encounter and can have problems with voices that are at a particular pitch. The AS adult will occasionally walk away rather than have to stay and listen to them talk.

Shouting and even talking in a loud voice, which they will label as shouting, can also be quite difficult for AS men to deal with. I often see the physical effect that talking loudly or shouting can have on an AS client in my consultation room. If a partner starts to raise her voice, I can often see his whole body tense up. If he displays AS traits in communication then these will worsen, for instance if he has problems with facial expression or eye contact, these will become exaggerated. His replies become less confident and will include many pauses, as his speech becomes more hesitant. It is important for the NT partner to recognize these signs; not just alone with her but in social groups too. Anxiety can be quite extreme in cases of Asperger syndrome, it can result in an anger outburst or complete withdrawal as he attempts to regain control of the situation and make the shouting stop.

Some of the men I spoke to would not socialize at all and refused point blank to go to social gatherings or entertain. They often said it made them feel uncomfortable and they did not know what to say or how to make small talk. Small talk and polite chitchat can be very difficult for the AS adult, as it often requires that the person speaking pretends to be interested in the other person. It might require talking about the weather or asking the other person what he or she does for a job. These trivialities are not important to AS adults and they would rather just talk about their own interests or converse with someone who shares their interests. One AS man once asked me why people always talked about the weather, 'I can see what the weather is like and so can they, why do we need to discuss and remind each other of something that we already know?'

Others do not feel they have a need to communicate with people who are irrelevant in their lives. Incentive and motivation play a huge part in whether AS adults will interact with another human being or not. If they are talking to someone they see as superior, relevant or as having a direct effect on their lives, then they will make some effort to interact. If however the other person is someone that they have nothing in common with and are unlikely to ever need for anything, then what is the point in talking to them? It is not about making the other person feel OK, welcomed or relevant because the AS adult does not perceive his or her feelings in this.

This is not to say the person with Asperger syndrome is totally selfish or narcissistic, because he is not, and this is not how he wishes to appear.

AS adults are only able to use logical thought to try and interpret an illogical society that has some very strange rules. The AS man does not naturally know these rules; he can be told about them and try to learn and adapt, but this will not come naturally. Our complex society is full of double meanings, sarcasm, unspoken rules, hidden agendas and a whole maze of subtle silent interactions, and it is difficult for the AS adult to cope with social situations and the stress and anxiety it puts him under. If he does not make a beeline for the nearest exit, then he may disappear into a corner, or become quite loud and interrupt conversations to try and exercise some control over what is being said. Both reactions are the AS man's way of coping and trying to deal with the situation he has found himself in.

Twenty per cent of the AS men expressed the desire to be liked and accepted by others. They can become aware that it is they who do not seem to get it right and the constant failures to be accepted can cause depression and isolation, especially in adolescents. It is important for parents to be aware and to watch out for this happening; trying to arrange for their teenager to receive the appropriate help and support may make a substantial difference. Parents may find themselves having to advise and inform their child on the difficulties and dangers that can occur in social situations.

Likewise it is often the partner who ends up being the social guide and will find herself constantly on the look out for those risky situations and embarrassing moments when she needs to rush in and save the situation. Many say they feel as though they have another child, and the responsibility can wear them down. Although the AS partner can be quite protective of her, he may not realize that his actions and behaviour can actually put her at risk.

One couple on holiday in America was visiting New York. The AS partner had a problem with adolescents who wore baseball caps, especially if they were worn with the peak at the back instead of the front. The couple were on the subway and between the start and end of their journey; the train stopped at the Bronx, an area particularly notorious for muggings and trouble. Before they even got on the train he had spotted a group of teenagers; two of the group were wearing baseball caps the wrong way. He instantly grabbed his wife's arm and as the train approached, held it very tightly. The train stopped, he held her back while the group boarded the train, and then he pushed her quickly into another carriage.

What he did not realize was that the teenagers could commute between carriages and they did just that, ending up in the same carriage as the couple. He was so tense he just stared at them. They noticed his unwanted attention and challenged it by asking him what he thought he was looking at. 'You,' he answered and then told them if they did not keep away he would report them to the police. This went down like a ton of bricks! They started to jeer and mock; he reacted to this with anger and would not back down. He did not realize the danger he was putting himself and his wife in, all he could see was a group of youths in baseball caps. Luckily the couple arrived at their destination and she steered him off the train. She was in a terrible state and had been frightened that someone would pull a knife on them, or worse. He had not even considered this and was not aware of how frightened she was. His single focus and inability to see the consequence of his actions had taken over.

It often appears that when an AS adult gets an idea into his head, he goes onto automatic pilot and nothing can stop him reaching his objective. This can be a huge plus if it is directed into a competitive sport such as marathon running or if it is a focus on an important project at work. But if that focus turns itself towards a more negative goal it can be very destructive for all those around. For instance, one man's focus became his daughter's boyfriend when he decided he did not like him. It was as though this father's mission was to eliminate the boyfriend and he made his and his daughter's life very difficult. The father believed that he had her best interests at heart and that she would be better off without her boyfriend. A dislike such as this could be based on all manner of reasons, from the colour of his hair to the car he drives, or even his name.

It is said that AS adults do not discriminate against race, age or sex and in some cases this is accurate, but it is not always so. I have heard accounts of people with Asperger syndrome being very rude to others because of their nationality, their colour or the fact they smoked or belonged to a particular group. The memory of the person with AS can be quite selective and if he is wronged in a way that affects him directly he will never forget certain aspects of it. Take, for instance, the man who did not like anyone in a baseball cap worn back to front. When I talked to him it became obvious where these feeling of mistrust and dislike came from.

When he had lived alone before getting married, he had been agitated by a group of youths that hung around drinking and being noisy in the entry that ran parallel to his house. Their noise disturbed him and kept him awake. One night he heard them and was watching them out of his bedroom window when he saw one of them throw an empty beer can over his fence and into his garden. This in his mind meant war. He grabbed his jeans (that was all he was wearing) and ran out of the house in pursuit of this gang. They were shocked and at first took flight, but he was a good runner and caught one of them up, cornering him. The youth attacked him and his friends joined in; he was severely beaten up and was admitted to the hospital with many bruises, a broken nose and fractured ribs from the kicking he had taken. The youths were wearing baseball caps back to front. This had stayed in his mind ever since and as soon as he saw anyone in a baseball cap worn back to front he perceived them to be the same as the youths that had so badly beaten him up.

Socializing does seem to cause most AS adults problems in one way or another. These problems will be very different according to the in-dividual's potential for socializing, his upbringing and how much he have been affected by Asperger syndrome. We are all different when it comes to socializing, some are better at it than others, some people can just captivate an audience and some have to work hard to refine their social skills and abilities. Other people do not want to socialize, they are happy to stay in, watch the TV or get on with their particular interest. There is no set rule in being good at socializing whether or not someone has Asperger syndrome. If you take a person who is a natural at socializing and give him Asperger Syndrome, the disabilities associated with AS will not be as pronounced in him and his life will be easier because he inherently possesses strong social skills. If you take a person who does not like, want or finds it difficult to socialize and give him Asperger syndrome, he may be a complete recluse. It is all to do with original potential and individuality.

The next factor to affect socializing ability is upbringing: some families are very sociable and open and others are very private and closed. One AS man I spoke to was brought up in a large Irish family whose front door was always open and where there was always food cooking on the stove. He had benefited hugely from this friendly sociable family unit and he was more able to cope with family gatherings and social events. I have also met AS men who grew up as only children and where it was very likely that one parent, if not both, was also on the autistic spectrum. Their upbringings were quite solitary and insular. I spoke to one man from such a family upbringing and he talked about how protective his parents were of him and how he was bought all the presents he could wish for. He would sit there at Christmas surrounded by all these wonderful presents, games, building blocks and train sets. The trouble was that he was never allowed any friends around to play with him. Consequently, he had tremendous problems socializing and learning to share. This was very apparent in his relationship with his partner and their children, he just could not participate in anything they did unless it was of interest to him and he had arranged it. It may be that these men had different potentials for socializing, but it is very likely that their upbringing either hindered or helped whatever that original potential was. Upbringing can affect how we relate to people whether we have AS or not. Early intervention is very important in Asperger syndrome and appropriate education in social abilities does make a difference.

The other deciding factor in the degree to which the socializing ability is affected by AS, is whether this is the area that is most disabled. Three core areas are influenced by AS and it is not the case that the difficulties will be equally divided between them: one-third communication, one-third social relationships and the remaining third in imagination. The distribution of effect varies greatly and in some cases may be only twenty per cent social relationships, and in other cases fifty per cent. This is what makes Asperger syndrome so difficult to diagnose and detect; it is complex, individual and does not abide by any particular set of rules.

Women with Asperger syndrome varied greatly in their answers, some felt quite capable and able to socialize, but put this down to having a very open and sociable upbringing. Sixty per cent expressed difficulty in socializing in large groups. Some felt it almost impossible to socialize and preferred to stay away from social groups or gatherings. Wanting to eat only particular foods and often only foods prepared by themselves also caused problems when socializing. In my research women with AS seemed to not show any advantage in socializing over men with AS, although they did appear to try a lot harder to be accepted.

Key points

- Sometimes it is only the NT partner's sense of humour that helps the couple survive awkward social situations.

- Some AS adults say they have no problems socializing, but more choose not to socialize.

- Individuals with AS appear to be affected at different levels in their socializing ability.

- Some AS men complain that their partners accuse them of being rude to others.

- Most AS men are simply being honest and are unaware of the social rules of politeness.

- The AS adult may often be aware they feel uncomfortable in a social situation, but not realize why.

- Adults with Asperger syndrome do not always experience feelings of embarrassment.

- Sometimes AS adults will see no reason to communicate with a person they perceive as irrelevant.

- Some AS men express the desire to be liked and accepted by others.

- There are times when the AS adult may not realize that his actions potentially expose his partner to risk.

- Personality and upbringing can make a difference to the AS adult's social needs and abilities.

- Most AS women feel able to socialize but experience difficulty in large groups.

11

Routines, Rules and Boundaries

The need for rules and routines has been identified as one of the traits caused by having Asperger syndrome. This often comes under the heading of 'imagination' when describing Asperger syndrome, the third core area affected by the syndrome. Many men and women with AS have argued that they have a perfectly good imagination, but this comes down to a question of definition. If someone is unable to see the colour red he does not know it exists and will argue he can see colour, or a colour that he perceives to be red, perfectly well.

When AS children are given toys to play with they will often put them into an order or sequence. One young boy when given a box of toy cars carefully placed them in a line, saying that he was putting them in order. The cars appeared to be completely disorganized; different shapes and colours all irregularly lined up. His mother asked him what sort of order they were in and he said they were in alphabetical order according to the make of the car, so an Austin Mini was first, followed by a BMW and so on. Quite impressive for an eight-year-old! Adults with Asperger syndrome also attempt to bring some order to their lives, it may be meal times, bed time or an irrelevancy that makes little sense to anyone but them. All the routines though will have a common theme or thread, whatever it is, it will be about control.

Control is usually an essential requirement for the AS adult to maintain his life and keep some order in it. If you can imagine living in a world that is confusing, complex and totally unpredictable, you will realize why some control is essential for the AS adult, who is constantly striving to survive in this confusing world with only half a bag of tools in his social skills kit. This causes stress and anxiety, so he tries to reduce this by bringing in rules and routines that he does not have to interpret or think about, he can just do them automatically. This is vital to relieve pressure and anxiety, it is as therapeutic to the AS adult as a back massage or a glass of wine. It is a way of winding down without having to think, talk or analyse, just going through the motions in the same way, rarely making any changes to the schema.

It is this inflexibility that can cause the problems in a relationship. The routines can become so rigid and necessary that he will not change them to fit the context and everyone in the household will have to conform to his routine. If a family member does not conform, the consequences of rebelling and retaliating can outweigh the gain. This can cause problems in some families, but a lot depends on what form the particular routine takes and what it involves. For instance, if it is checking all the doors are locked at night this can be useful, if, however, it is dinner on the table at exactly six o'clock every evening regardless of whether one of the kids need a lift to town or there is a parents' evening on, it can cause severe problems.

One woman's life was totally dominated by her husband's rigid and strict routines. Every night he would position his five alarm clocks in exactly the same places, checking them in the same order. Two of the clocks rang, one was a radio alarm, another buzzed, and the fifth one had a flashing light. He would set them all for different times and when he was happy they were all set correctly he would say goodnight to his wife and turn off the light, she was not allowed to stay awake longer then he. At exactly 6.15 a.m. a bell rang, at 6.20 a.m. a buzzer went off, at 6.25 a.m. another bell rang, at 6.30 a.m. the radio came on with the news and if by then she had not gone totally crazy the light started flashing at 6.35 a.m.. At this point he got up, put on his slippers and dressing gown and went downstairs, leaving his wife with the radio blaring away some awful song and the light flashing on the bedside table. He would have his breakfast, always cornflakes, and make a pot of tea. She stayed upstairs while he had breakfast. He would get very agitated if she got up and also came downstairs. When he had finished breakfast he would come back upstairs, give her a cup of tea and then clean his teeth. Cleaning his teeth was a work of art and he was meticulous about it, as he was about all bodily cleanliness. He would then shower and dress, checking the creases in his trousers and adjusting his tie. At precisely 7.30 a.m. he would say 'Well, I will be off now, goodbye,' and go out of the front door. He would walk around his car on the drive to check it was OK, stopping to stare at every little speck on it, and then leave.

He returned in the evening at exactly 7.00 p.m., unless there was a problem with the roads or traffic. He would have a shower and be seated at the table by 7.30 p.m. expecting his dinner to be ready. If not, he would get very agitated and make some critical comment like 'Have you been wasting time on the phone to your mother again?' He had specific foods he liked which could only be cooked in a certain way. If his wife ran out of one of these foods or forgot to buy it he would react quite angrily. She discovered his annoyance if she got it wrong quite early on in the relationship. He liked fresh broccoli with his meals and expected this on Monday, Wednesday and Friday. One Monday she had fetched the broccoli from the vegetable rack and discovered it had turned yellow over the weekend. Without so much as a thought she gave him peas instead. When she handed him his dinner he just sat there staring at his plate, in total disbelief.

'Why have you given me peas, why haven't you given me broccoli?'

Just the way he spoke and looked at her reduced her to tears.

After that she made sure that he always had his fresh broccoli on the nominated days. It was very sad that his routines had been allowed to become so fixed and inflexible. When they had first married, his young wife had tried very hard to please him and do things for him, like his mother had. He was an only child and very spoilt, she on the other hand had experienced a very emotionally abusive childhood, and her father had been very loud and aggressive. She had accepted her husband's dominance and he had taken total control.

Asperger syndrome is a developmental condition and this can impede emotional maturity. If we were to put a child in total control of our lives and allow him to always get his own way, and then fail to meet the child's needs, the child would probably react by having a temper tantrum. AS anger can present itself like a child's tantrum, it will erupt, cause a lot of stress to those around and then disappear. The AS person will often not be aware of the devastation and emotional pain their over-reaction has caused others.

Considering the frequency of routines and rules amongst adults with Asperger syndrome it was initially surprising that sixty-five per cent in my study said they did not have any routines or fixed ways. What their NT partners said, though, was quite different when they talked about their partners' various routines. The most common was the 'locking up' routine: all doors would be checked in a definite order; if a door were already closed it would be opened and then closed again. Then there was the 'shopping routine' which included specific ways of shopping, such as lining up the cans on the checkout counter and packing things very specifically; tying up every single plastic carrier bag in a way that made it impossible to open safely without a pair of scissors; finally replacing the trolley very precisely with the other trolleys. Supermarkets seem to be one of the few places where AS men feel they can behave like children again and a few have been known to take a ride on the trolley, whizzing up and down the aisles completely oblivious to shoppers around them.

Many jobs and chores will have their own specific script, even putting a shelf on the wall. One man did this to perfection and was very particular about any bits of plaster falling onto the floor when he drilled, making his wife or one of the children stand with a dustpan under the hole he was drilling. He could have put paper or a sheet on the floor, but he argued quite correctly that the dust would land on the wall. It would be very tiring for the dustpan holder because he would take so long, measuring the hole size and position exactly, lining up the holes, stopping, lining them up again and on and on. Yes, the end result would be a perfectly placed symmetrical and balanced shelf that an elephant could sit on without causing it to give way, and one very frustrated near-to-screaming partner or child who had been forced to take part in the whole time-consuming exercise.

Outings and excursions can also become fixed and one man reported how he liked to go to the same places when the family went out for the day. He said it felt safe because he knew what to expect. This reflects how confusing and complex the world can appear to someone with Asperger syndrome. Difficulty in reading both people and situations and the extra pressure and stress it can cause can leave little room for anticipating what a new place is going to be like. Will it be welcoming, convenient, uncomplicated, or will it require much thought and be fraught with complications and complexities? Will it be a total disaster, will he get it wrong, will he disappoint and let the whole family down, and will his partner get angry with him? Many thoughts and anxieties such as these will go through the AS man's mind; many fears will prevent him from experimenting with something new.

This man was very aware that the family wanted to go somewhere else. He knew that they were bored and tired with going to the same place, but the thought of exploring new avenues and being responsible for the consequences was probably more than he could tolerate.

Asperger syndrome and chaos do not go well together: the AS person can be very good at causing it, but not very good at resolving the chaos when the situation is not in his control. The AS brain is constantly trying to interpret what must seem like a foreign language spoken by a foreign culture in a foreign land. If the AS man chooses to stick with the tried and tested, the unknown aspect is immediately solved and he can better predict and stay in control of any unexpected situations that may arise. This does not, however, make the day less boring and uneventful for everyone else.

Another area that can become fixed by routine is the sexual act. This was mentioned for the most part by the NT partner, who said it left her feeling used and unloved. I will talk more about this in Chapter 13.

Several AS men confessed that they needed their routines to help them keep things in control because it was a method of stabilizing their lives and maintaining a semblance of order. Many were also aware that it frustrated and irritated their partners but still felt unable to change the patterns they had established.

One man said he needed to be in control and if challenged he would become angry towards his partner until she gave in. He was obsessive about time and his life was quite dominated by it. He could not be late; neither would he allow anyone else in his family to be late. Long before the time they were due to go somewhere he would be looking at his watch or one of the many clocks he had filled his house with, and remind his partner that they had to be there in one and a half hours time. He would ask her to tell him what she was going to do in that time, he would then ask the kids the same questions. Ten minutes later he would be checking that she was doing the things she said she would. He would calculate the time it would take her for each task and then check she was running to schedule, constantly looking at his watch and reminding her that they had only so many minutes left. They would all be very frustrated and wound up by the time they left. Tempers would be high; he would drive too fast and get quite loud and abusive with the rest of the family. He could not see the negative effect this had on everyone, all he could see was the time and the importance to him that they should arrive on time.

This obsessive behaviour can be focused on many different things, for quite a few AS men it was table etiquette. This can make meal times miserable for the family members concerned. One man had a very fixed idea of how his family should eat their meals, use a knife and fork and sit at the table. The family would sit down together for a meal and he would instantly focus on their four-year-old. He would get up from the table and push his son's chair closer to the table; he would then adjust the knife and fork in his hands, sit down and watch him. The atmosphere would be so tense, the boy would not get it right and forget to use his knife or wiggle his chair back from the table, and so the battle between father and son continued. Mum would become protective and defensive and say something that diverted her husband's attention to her. She would accuse him of being a snob or picking on the kids, he would retaliate and say he was only doing what was best for her son, arguing that she did not care if he got picked on at school because he did not know how to eat properly. He questioned what sort of mother she was who did not care how her children ate at the table and on and on it went. Nothing would budge him from his rules on table etiquette. There were times when he would agree with his wife to keep quiet and just let them get on with it, but the second they sat at the table he went into automatic pilot and it began all over again. It was as though he had no control over the way he behaved at meal times. Meal times became a constant battleground and in the end mum arranged them separately, so that the kids ate first before dad came home and then the two of them ate together later.

This obsessive behaviour probably has its roots in childhood; this particular man went to a public school, which was very strict. For other men I have spoken to this obsessive behaviour was established during adolescence when they were desperately trying to be popular. They developed the notion that table manners were a passport to being accepted and asked round to friends' houses. This idea may become totally exaggerated and out of proportion as the behaviour is practised to perfection. Consequently when a partnership or family is later formed, everyone else is expected to conform and follow the same pattern. This can be very difficult for children, especially young children who do not have the motor skills to eat perfectly with a knife and fork, and in the case of older children there is the possibility that they will rebel.

Whether individuals had routines, why they needed them, and how aware they were of the effect their routine had on others, varied quite drastically among AS men. Why it varied may be dependent on the individuals' own basic nature and how much was allowed by their parents and later their partners.

Partners need to be very direct and objective when discussing change. The argument has to be presented to their AS partners in an unemotional way, otherwise the message will not be heard and retained. Routines can be restricted or altered although rarely stopped altogether. It is far better though not to let them become fixed in the first place and certainly not to initially conform to try to please or pacify an AS partner.

If the couple are both aware of the presence of Asperger syndrome and understand the effect it has, it can make a tremendous difference. Issues can be dealt with in a more appropriate way that will not cause the AS partner to feel under attack and criticized when his partner raises the question of changing the routine.

Many AS men said they had found it easier to recognize and try to change some of their routines since they discovered that Asperger syndrome was the cause. Awareness of Asperger syndrome can make quite a difference to how an individual and especially a couple will manage and cope with some of the problematic aspects of their relationship. This subject is so huge that I have dedicated a whole chapter to it (18 Asperger Syndrome and Awareness).

AS women were not very different to AS men when it came to routines and rules. Some initially said that they did not have any, but later admitted certain rules and regimes they had developed regarding cleaning the house, and rules the rest of the family had to follow, like folding towels and making their beds in a certain way.

To sum up, obsessive and rigid routines did not cause the AS person any difficulties, it was how they affected his partner and children that caused problems and in some cases made the family's life miserable. Obsessions are just one of the problems that can affect parenting and childcare by families when one parent or both have Asperger syndrome.

Key points

- Adults with AS need to have some order in their lives.

- AS adults' routines are often about control.

- These routines can become very rigid, regimented and inflexible.

- It can happen that an NT woman's life is completely controlled by her partner's routines.

- Most AS men claim they do not have any particular routines.

- Household jobs and chores are often performed in a specific way by AS adults.

- AS adults' holidays and excursions may become fixed and unvaried.

- Routines and rules can make families' lives miserable.

- NT partners need to stop routines from becoming fixed, once they are aware of them.

- AS women have the same need for routine as AS men.

12

The Asperger Syndrome Parent

Questions have been raised about whether a parent with Asperger syndrome is a good enough parent. The implication behind these questions is vast and this chapter is not about judgement or evaluating the suitability and capability of an AS parent. It simply presents the findings that my research uncovered.

Having Asperger syndrome does not make a person a bad parent, any more than not having Asperger syndrome makes a person a good parent. How anyone performs as a parent is determined by a whole host of variables:

- What kind of childhood did the person have, was it abusive in any way?

- Was their upbringing consistent? Was love unconditional?

- What are the person's individual traits? Are they naturally maternal or paternal?

- Are they quick-tempered or placid, introvert or extrovert by nature?

- How much harmony is there in the home, what are the pressures and stresses?

- Is the family financially secure?

- Was the child planned and wanted?

- Did the parents specifically want a boy or a girl?
- Is the child a biological child, stepchild or adopted?

All these questions and many more need to be considered before the presence of Asperger syndrome alone is blamed for the breakdown of the family relationship. Yes, having Asperger syndrome will make a difference, and if that difference is negative and the bond between that parent and child is weak then Asperger syndrome can exaggerate these problems. If, though, the bond is strong and the parent is motivated and wants to be a good parent, and both parent and child are aware that Asperger syndrome is the cause of some of the difficulties, then the parenting can be good enough.

Unfortunately, even with the best intention in the world, having Asperger syndrome and children can present problems and it is this area of the family system that often causes the AS parent more concern and stress than any other. Understanding, predicting and interacting with other adults can cause a high stress level in the AS adult. Children are even more complex and so unpredictable that the AS father will find relating and interacting with his children stressful and difficult at times.

The anxiety and stress voiced by many fathers with Asperger syndrome seems to begin long before the baby is born and many of them talked about the worry this caused them and the concerns they had. One man discussed how afraid and anxious he was about the impending birth of their son, he talked about his feelings of uncertainty and his fear of failure as a father. He worried constantly about whether his son would like him, whether he would be able to support him and show him he cared. He did not express these fears to his wife at the time and instead became very quiet and withdrawn. His wife explained to me how sensitive he was to criticism at this time and how every time she talked about the baby he found some way of hearing what she was saying as a criticism against him. For example, she once asked him if he was pleased they were having a son or would he have preferred a daughter (this couple knew in advance the sex of their child). He went instantly on the defensive and replied, 'Why are you asking me that? Do you think I will not be any good with a boy? Are you trying to say I am not a very good role model for a boy?'

A simple question that only sought the reassurance she needed soon turned into a very unnecessary row. If he had explained to her how he felt, she might have understood and been able to deal better with his fears. Instead it just felt to her that he was constantly picking on every thing she said and did. She read his reaction as him not wanting the child and she in turn built up her walls and withdrew from him. The pregnancy was turning out to be a very unhappy time for both of them, each misreading the situation and making assumptions about what the other partner felt. Communication broke down and the marriage was suffering at a time when they should have been growing together. It was only when they came to counselling that he spoke about his real fears and how he had been so scared that he was going to let her and the baby down.

When these issues were sorted out and a better understanding between the couple developed, their relationship began to strengthen and, although the problems did not end there, he was at least able to voice his fearful feelings and she was able to reassure him that he was doing just fine.

Another man whose wife was pregnant said he was concerned that he would not be able to feel any love for his unborn child. He struggled with the idea that he would be expected to have feelings for a child he did not know. This is due to the lack of imaginative thought shown by people with Asperger syndrome. It is extremely difficult for them to imagine a child that does not yet exist and imagine having automatic feelings of love for it. These fears often disappear once the child is born and becomes real to them.

After the birth problems may take on a different form. Many NT women complained that they were the ones who took all the responsibility for the childcare and rearing of the children and this was true in most situations.

The children of AS parents have often described them as distant, quiet and unemotional. If the AS parent is the father, the effect on the child does not seem to be as extreme as when it is the mother, who is often expected to be the close, caring and emotional figure in the family. Mothers are often expected to be excellent mind readers, always knowing exactly what her children think and want before they do. Trying to fulfil this role and having Asperger syndrome has caused extreme anxiety for some mums, especially before they discovered that they had AS. Being aware of AS and the difficulties it causes often makes a huge difference in the way the person feels about themselves and the way they interact with the rest of the family.

One woman described her life before being diagnosed with Asperger syndrome as a complete nightmare; she was trying to be a good enough mum to four children and this left her feeling ragged, depressed and exhausted. She tried to compensate for what she felt she could not offer them emotionally by doing practical things for them. Her daughter, now grown up, told me how she remembered when she had come home from school sobbing her heart out, because the class bully had picked on her. Her mum did not ask what she was crying about; she just rushed out to the newsagents to buy her a comic and a chocolate bar. She had simply focused on stopping her daughter crying so they could get on with their usual daily routine. Her daughter described how her mother would try to get it right and when she failed she would, at times react with frustration and anger. It influenced the children in different ways; the two girls were very resentful that their upbringing was so lacking in what they perceived should have been a mother's love. All the comics and chocolate bars in the world could not compensate for that. The two sons, however, did not feel they had suffered or been deprived in any way.

Being a mother with Asperger syndrome seems to present more difficulties than being a father with AS. This may simply be due to society's perceptions of the roles of mother and father. Mother is supposed to be warm, empathetic, intuitive, insightful, psychic, loving, caring and much more. Father is supposed to be provider, protector, somewhat distant, in control and disciplinary. These roles are changing now in Western society, but fifty years ago would have been quite traditional and rigid and being an AS father then would have probably been accepted as standard behaviour. Men were not expected to be present at the birth, feed and change the baby, they were not expected to participate in play, take children to the clinic or spend much time with them. That was all mother's job. These roles still hold true in some cultures and indeed in some relationships today. I think it can be said that, even in today's society, in many cases men are put under a lot less pressure to be nurturers in the family than women are.

Quite a few AS women do not have children because they have decided early on that they did not want to, even if that meant not having sex, as one woman described. It appears that for some AS women maternal feelings are not very strong. This may be due to the lack of imagination mentioned earlier, she just cannot imagine automatically loving and caring for a child she has not yet had.

In one relationship where the mother has Asperger syndrome, the father had taken over the maternal role and gave out the TLC (tender loving care) when the children needed it. This man had strong autistic traits and it had not been easy for him. He appears to have done a brilliant job and his children are very close to him. His wife at one stage in the children's early teens had decided to return to study and actually moved into digs while she took her MA at a university 500 miles away.

As the majority of AS parents in this study are men it is the role of the father that my studies focused on. Thirty-six per cent of the AS fathers said that they had a good relationship with their biological children. The majority, however, said they often felt despair and sometimes annoyance at the problems that fatherhood had brought them. Most of the fathers in my study wanted to be close to their children and form an attachment with them, but also seemed to be at a total loss as to what they should do to achieve this. One man said he just could not think of how to play with his daughter. He could not think of anything fun to do; he would try to initiate a game with her, but it normally ended up being played in his way according to his rules as he could not adapt to her needs or her level of development.

A father with Asperger syndrome often struggles with adapting to the age of the child and the maturity levels that child is operating at. They will at times talk to and treat their young children as though they were adults. This again is due to the difficulty people with Asperger syndrome have trying to infer another person's mental state. Understanding children is even harder and it is almost impossible for an AS adult to think empathetically on a child's emotional and intellectual level. This can cause his expectations of the child to far exceed the child's capabilities, putting excessive pressure on the child to live up to unreasonable expectations and perform at a higher level than he or she is mentally capable of.

For example, one father was particularly eager for his son to learn to ride a bike because he liked riding his own bike and saw it as a recreation they could do together. He bought his son a bike as soon as he considered him physically big enough to ride one. That same afternoon he put the bike in the back of the car and went off with his son. When they returned their son was in a dreadful state, he sobbed and cried.

'What on earth has gone on?' his mum asked.

Her husband was very angry and wound up. 'I took him up to Witts Hill and he just whinged and would not even try to ride his bike! Complete waste of a good bike!'

Now, Witts Hill is a fantastic place for kids to cycle on. It is full of very steep mounds and is really great if you are over ten and have a BMX. It's not so great though if you are four years old and expected to cycle without stabilizers, as the father had taken these off. He had shouted and bullied his son and had taken the view that his son was being awkward and ungrateful. He thought he was doing the best for his son and wanted him to enjoy the experience that he himself would have enjoyed. He could not see the damage he was doing and his son never did take to cycling after that.

Pressure to score academically can also become a major problem. One young woman whose father had Asperger syndrome wrote:

> When I was at school we did not know Dad had Asperger syndrome, we knew he had some odd ways but thought that was just the way he was. When you are a kid you don't question the way your parents are, you just accept it. When I was doing my GCSE's it was all my dad talked to me about, every time he saw me he asked if I was doing my revision. I was not allowed to go out or have any fun. I achieved eight As and one B in chemistry. I thought I had done really well. When I told my dad he just stood there, saying 'You only got a B in chemistry, you only got a B, I am so disappointed in you, I expected better'. I will never forget his words, all the pressure of trying so hard to please him and then to be told I had disappointed him. I can still feel the way that day affected me – it still makes me feel sick inside.

Life for a child being raised in an AS environment can be extremely stressful. There are so many pressures brought to bear upon them – pressure to achieve in education, pressure to eat in the socially correct way, pressure to dress in a manner perceived to be acceptable – the list is endless. In the eyes of the AS father, he is doing his best but is oblivious of the damage he is causing his child's self-esteem. This is where family life can become a battleground and mum may attempt to protect and defend her children against this very authoritarian and controlling parenting style. If it is not recognized that Asperger syndrome is present it can become a nightmare for all the family.

Not all AS fathers are overly critical and distant and some women have described their AS husbands as being totally soft with their kids. One man with Asperger syndrome said that he loved his kids more than life itself. This was a man who recognized he had Asperger syndrome and was willing to let his wife guide him when he was unsure what to do. She had learned to deliver this guidance in a way that did not seem critical or attacking.

Many women report concern for their children's welfare when the AS father is left in charge. This is not because they think the father will abuse or intentionally hurt them, but because they feel he is not able to be fully responsible for them. The NT women in my research said almost collectively that they felt they had an extra child to look after, and some said that is exactly how it feels when they leave their partner's in charge of their children; it is like leaving their children in the care of another child – a child who is likely to get side-tracked or totally absorbed in another subject matter, or a child who would panic if something went wrong and he did not know what to do. They know their partners will do their best, but that best does not always work for the child.

Problems caused by their partners getting side-tracked or distracted was an issue raised by quite a few of the NT mothers. This was not just in relation to when he was caring for the children; it is a problem that can arise at the most unexpected times. Sometimes it can occur when he is supposed to be dealing with an important subject when he may, without warning, focus on what might appear quite a minor and irrelevant concern. This can be impossible to divert – once his focus has switched, his whole line of thought and communication will be directed onto this particular issue.

One couple had been called in to school to discuss an issue that had arisen over their son. While they were both talking to the teacher, her husband suddenly jumped up from his seat and walked over to the wall. Up on the wall were pictures and drawings of tanks that the children had put together. There was a picture of one tank that underneath said Panzer 111F. Her husband pointed out that it was totally incorrect, he said that is a Panzer 111G, and it had a longer gun than the Panzer F. The teacher said he was sure it could not be wrong. Her husband argued relentlessly that he was correct and the caption was, in fact erroneous. His single focused quest needed to be satisfactorily concluded and the only way forward was to seek the information on the reverse of the photo. Before anyone could speak he had taken the picture down and disrupted the whole display. 'I knew it!' he exclaimed, 'It is a Panzer G, maybe I had better check the other pictures too.' Ten minutes later, the teacher was getting quite impatient whilst trying to stay polite as the husband had now got embroiled in his favourite subject and the teacher was slowly being taught all there was to know about tanks. His wife felt shown up and embarrassed as they were supposed to be talking about their son. Her husband's focus had diverted, he was an expert on tanks and nothing was going to stop him until he had proved his point. This is when that single focus can get in the way and it may be almost impossible to divert until the mission is accomplished.

This single focus can also prevent the AS man from being totally aware of what is going on around him as one woman found out when she left her husband in charge of their seven-year-old son. Her husband had bought their son a Playstation and was going to set it up that evening while she was out at a Neighbourhood Watch meeting. She felt relieved that at least she was leaving him working in a sphere that he enjoyed and pictured father and son playing together on the Playstation. She had not thought to check that the games he had bought could be set up for more than one person!

Yes, dad had set the Playstation up and started playing on it, and he played and played. When she came home her son was in a flood of tears lying downstairs on the settee, while dad played upstairs completely absorbed in the game and not even concerned that his son had not had a go on it. When she asked him how he could be so selfish, he said only one person could play on it at a time and anyway his son had gone off so obviously did not want to play anyway. His son had 'gone off' after he had stood around for nearly an hour watching dad enjoy himself!

Parenting can certainly present some problems for the AS family and my research found that these problems appear to be greatly exaggerated if the children are stepchildren. In every case I have encountered, problems with stepchildren seem to far outweigh the problems with biological children. Quite a few couples I have spoken to are second families and there are stepchildren involved. Either it is a second marriage for both of them or one or both have children from their first marriage, or the man with AS is marrying late and his chosen partner already has children, or she has been married before or is older than he.

Whatever the reasons, stepchildren and Asperger syndrome seem to have difficulty mixing together. Quite a few of the men I spoke to felt they had tried to get on with their stepchildren but had not been accepted by them or had been targeted or excluded by the children. Many quoted that they were only required for the practical things. One man said he was no more than a chauffeur, another claimed he was good enough to buy games and books for his stepchildren but no one wanted him to join in and play or read with them. Most men felt very unappreciated. Another man voiced this by saying he was completely irrelevant and of no importance whatsoever to his partner's teenage children. Some AS men can be very bound by their responsibility to their family and will often see it as their duty to see the father role through, this can change somewhat when the biological bond is not there and there is not the same sense of duty.

Parents with Asperger syndrome will often give and show love on a very practical level, they sort out a job that needs doing or they will offer to give a lift. However, what they offer will be very much on their terms and will be done in their way. One girl I spoke to whose stepfather had Asperger syndrome described a very typical instance.

> My stepfather was eating chocolate ice cream and my little brother wanted some. Instead of giving him chocolate he gave him a bowl of vanilla. My brother was upset and wanted chocolate like his stepdad. He said he could not have chocolate because there was more vanilla than chocolate in the freezer, he'd just had the chocolate himself and my brother had watched him eat it. My stepfather could not seem to see that what he had just done was so selfish, he just expected my brother to understand that he had to eat the vanilla ice-cream while his dad ate the chocolate.

This father had not realized how selfish his actions appeared and that rather than his own needs he should have been putting his stepson first. He was acting according to his needs rather than the child's and this does not make for a smooth parent-child relationship. Children can be quite egotistical and often selfish, and if child and adult are running on the same emotional level neither will want to put the other first. If you offer a child a bag of sweets he is unlikely to take the smallest one and leave you the biggest, putting your needs first; unfortunately neither will the AS adult. This is where problems can begin and the person who is going to end up right in the middle is mum. Some mums end up feeling absolutely torn apart, forced to take sides, often in defence of her children; child and adult will fight for her attention and she will not be able to please both.

Fighting for mum's attention can become a battleground, and can cause a lot of stress and anxiety for all involved. The more attention mum gives the children the more jealous and rejected the AS partner can feel, he can be quite vindictive and this will cause her to become more protective and defensive. One woman described how, time and time again she explained to her husband that the children had gone through enough in her previous relationship and he should act like the adult and not react every time they said something that he did not like. She tried to convince him that if he could just step back and give a bit of praise sometimes it would make so much difference to all concerned. He would listen, nod his head and agree to everything that she said. The problem would seem to be solved and go away until the next time something was said. He would go straight back into automatic pilot again and start to pick on the kids and make life difficult for all concerned.

The question this highlights is how does this affect the children? To find out I asked some children and adults how they felt being brought up by an AS parent had affected them. Here are two accounts that I have received. Names have been changed, but not the ages.

Caroline – 18

'It is really quite hard to know what to write as it's hard to separate the AS from what was just him, and to not feel like I'm just criticizing him. It was mainly the little incidents and things and then just a general attitude and behaviour really.

My stepdad was fanatical and strict about us having to do little things like pouring boiling water over plastic bottles to minimize the space in the bin. Another issue he was fanatical about was never using a knife that you had just used in the margarine in the jam – little things like that. I knew these made sense but his response to them at the time was completely irrational and out of context.

We would get told off for doing something with no rational justification and he was never able to bend or negotiate on what he said and the rules he made. He was never able to see our point of view.

If you asked him a question about an issue or subject that he was interested in, like his maps and planning routes, he would go on and on far beyond the realms of the question. For example when I asked him the way to point B... when my friend and I wanted to go on a short bike ride and he spent fifteen minutes describing every detail of the way – including every detail of the way we shouldn't go.

He used to get annoyed when we had friends round because we used to sit in the kitchen and talk; he said the noise disturbed him. He would often express his opinions about my friends out loud not seeming concerned whether my friends heard what he said or not. Once he made a comment about my friend who was going on holiday that caused quite a row between us. My friend had had her nose and lip pierced and wore a metal brace at the time. He said out loud in front of her, 'she's got so much metal in her face I will be surprised if she makes it through the detectors!' My friend was very hurt and embarrassed by this comment, so was I; I was really annoyed with him for being so rude.

If he had a complaint when we were out he would take it out on the shop staff, not appreciating that it was not their fault and they are just trying to do their job. He could not see that they were not responsible for his problem with the goods he had bought – he just didn't know when to stop, like he had to go out of his way and prove to them that he was right. He could not see the upset he caused people, he just had an objective to achieve. There were times when it would be over an issue that was completely irrelevant and made no difference to anything, he could not stop or let the subject drop.

Michael – 13

He did not spend any time doing fun things with me so mum used to get on at him to take me out; he started taking me to the cinema. When we got there though he would send me in on my own to see the film I wanted to watch and then he would go off and watch a film he wanted to watch. So we did not even spend that time together.

Sarah – 20

My mom married my stepdad when I was young so he is the only father I remember. My upbringing was quite bizarre and, although I did not realize at the time, it was quite different from how my friends grew up.

There were lots of things I wasn't allowed to do, like ever get my hands or clothes dirty or make too much noise. Meal times were the worst, they were so regimented.

I always felt criticized by my stepdad and not really loved for who I was, but rather for what I achieved. Yet at the same time I knew he would be there for me if I needed a hand fixing something or wanted a lift somewhere. He worked hard at his job and never forgot my birthday.

He was very protective when I started going out with boys and he could be quite rude to them and make them feel very uncomfortable.

Now I know he has Asperger syndrome it answers a lot of questions, I just wish someone had found out earlier, it could have saved a lot of tears, both for me and my mom.

I have included just a few accounts that I have received from children and young adults who have grown up in a family with a parent or stepparent who has Asperger syndrome. Many of them feel quite angry and let down that they did not receive any support or were not aware that one of their parents had Asperger syndrome.

Clearly this is an issue that needs to be addressed in the future, especially as general awareness of the syndrome increases. Support groups and specialized counselling should be available to these children as it is offered to other children in need. Talking to others who understand and can empathize with how they feel would help them feel more valued and not so alone.

The next area I look at is the sexual side of Asperger syndrome where loneliness can also be an issue.

Key points

- Having Asperger syndrome does not make a person a bad parent.
- Anxiety often begins in the AS father before the child is born.
- Children of parents with AS have described them as being distant, quiet and unemotional.
- AS parents can struggle very hard to be 'good enough' parents.
- Being an AS mother can present more difficulties than being an AS father.
- A number of AS fathers say they feel they have a good relationship with their biological children.
- AS parents can have difficulty adapting to the developmental age of the child.
- Many NT mothers say they feel they have an extra child in their care – the AS adult.
- An AS adult's liability to get sidetracked or distracted can cause problems in childcare.
- There can be extra difficulties if the children are the AS parent's stepchildren.

13

The Sexual Side
of Asperger Syndrome

How anyone relates to another person sexually is dependent on many factors, and sex can never be seen as a single issue. Upbringing, culture, religion, age, attitudes and, most importantly, the partner one is with can all affect sex. When I asked men with Asperger syndrome what attracted them to their partner, very few made references to anything of a sexual nature; it was far more about what she could offer in a practical sense. Most women described their AS partners as having been non-pushy, respectful and real gentlemen. Few felt in any way pressured to have sex and this came as a welcome change for many who felt they were living in a society which has lost some of the value that can be achieved by a slow courtship.

For many of the couples I spoke to, sex was not high on the agenda when they met, and most of the women regarded this as their new partner showing them respect and valuing them more as people than as sexual conquests. This played a very important role in the initial relationship formation between the couple.

One man told his future wife that he wanted to wait until they were married before they had sex; he was a virgin when they met and she can see in retrospect that, as he was in his forties, this should really have made her question why he was so sexually inexperienced. After two years they married and on the wedding night they attempted to make love. He was unable to get an erection due to being so anxious about his performance. He did not want their relationship to change and just could not relate to her in the sexual sense; their marriage was never consummated yet she stayed with him for twenty very frustrating years.

Sex is not always a problem in the Asperger relationship though, and some men find it the easiest way to communicate their deepest feelings and show their love for their partner. Sex is a form of communication; it is a way of expressing in a physical sense what we feel. I have been told by some AS men that they find this way of expressing their feelings far easier than trying to find the right words. For these men it is not just a sexual act, it is an act of love and it is kept exclusively for their chosen partners. They reinforce this by saying that without these feelings of love they would not be able to make love to their partner or any other woman.

Some couples have reported a very successful and caring sexual relationship. Most of the women in these cases were outgoing, quite confident sexually and some were already sexually experienced. This enabled the woman to take the lead and to be able to show her partner what she wanted and how to please her. If both are aware that he has Asperger syndrome and he is prepared to listen and learn from what she says, then sex will be even easier between them.

Sometimes though, his willingness to try and get it right can become obsessive. One man said he tried very hard to please his wife and thought he had achieved this, but then added that she complained he would not try anything different. I asked him why he did not want to try anything new and he replied, why try and improve something that was already exactly right? His wife had told him she was more than satisfied with their lovemaking and he felt it was good for him too. His focus was only on keeping things the same because for him it worked, he could not see that his wife needed some variation to the act. Yes, two years ago she had told him that she was satisfied but nothing had changed since then and she now wanted to try something different.

Another problem was making the first move; three of the men with Asperger syndrome said they found this very difficult. For the NT woman this can make her feel unwanted, and she may begin to doubt whether she actually turns him on. Many women in these situations felt this greatly affected their feelings of self-worth and confidence, which is understandable if they were always having to initiate sex and were then left wondering if he really wanted them or was simply obliging them by making love in return. When I spoke to the men in these situations I found that in many cases the men also felt they were unwanted and undeserving. They wanted to please their wives but felt unable or not confident enough to initiate sex. One reason for this is probably the difficulty people with Asperger syndrome have in reading the non-verbal signs given by their partner. One man said he found it impossible to guess when his wife wanted sex and when she only wanted a cuddle; he said he had got it wrong many times and thought she had wanted him to make love to her when she did not. He said now he did not try for fear he would get it wrong and be accused of only ever thinking about one thing. He said that he could not understand why his partner could not simply tell him she wanted intercourse, or if she wanted to have an orgasm, or if she was on her period so just wanted a cuddle and no more. He asked how was he supposed to guess when nine times out of ten he would probably get it wrong and then she would accuse him of being selfish or insensitive.

Reading what his partner wants from him is difficult in any situation for the adult with Asperger syndrome. In bed it is even more difficult as there is often a lack of verbal communication, which makes it even harder for him to know what she wants. Difficulty in reading the signs from his partner can sometimes lead him to believe that his partner wants sex when she does not. This could result in him trying to take things too far and then he could find himself accused of being pushy; even worse he could be accused of attempted rape or rape itself, if the message 'no sex' is not given loud and clear.

This is one of the reasons why it is essential that adolescents with Asperger syndrome should be taught very clearly and directly some of the rules about sexual conduct and that 'No' can be voiced in more ways than the spoken word. Standard mainstream school sex education is not enough for teenagers with Asperger syndrome and all the issues surrounding attraction, dating courtship and sex need to be broken down into segments and explained in far more specific detail than is currently being offered in schools.

A teenage boy I spoke to believed that if a girl let him touch her breasts that meant she would also allow him to have intercourse with her. This belief was simply based on what he had observed on TV. He needed clear instructions about what he should do and say in intimate sexual situations.

It is less likely that a young teenage girl will be vocal about what she wants, it is more likely that she will try to convey to him through her body language that she does not want sex. For instance, rather than saying 'do not touch me there', she may try to move her body in a way that makes it difficult for him to touch her. He may not understand this, as reading body language is already an area he struggles with. He will need to be taught about the mysteries of courtship and sex, and given very clear directions.

Likewise it is important the teenager with Asperger syndrome is not put under pressure to have sex in order to be popular with his peers and to gain street credit in front of his friends. He will probably notice that the popular kids are the ones that score and he might attempt to copy them, when in fact he neither wants nor feels ready to have a sexual encounter.

Feeling pressured to perform sexually also concerned three of the AS men I spoke to. Some said that their partners demanded sex at certain times of the month and they were expected to know when these times were and perform accordingly. Others complained that there were certain aspects of sex they felt very uncomfortable with such as oral sex. Despite this they still felt pressured into performing the act. For these men it was likely that they would stop having sex altogether or find that being pressured into an involuntary action would compromise their ability to achieve an erection.

Twenty six per cent of the AS men complained that sex was not frequent enough and wanted a more active sex life, which might indicate that most of the AS men were sexually active. However, approximately fifty per cent of the women I spoke to said that there was no sexual contact in the relationship with their AS partner.

Some professionals might argue that this is a natural consequence of Asperger syndrome. This is a false belief, resulting from Asperger syndrome being so closely linked with cases of classic autism. The film *Rain Man* reinforced this view quite strongly; it showed clearly that Raymond (played by Dustin Hoffman) had no sexual interests whatsoever. Autism can cause an individual to be very insular and withdrawn, often not communicating and certainly not interested in close physical contact. This though does not apply accurately to Asperger syndrome and to view all those with Asperger syndrome as being non-sexual would be quite erroneous.

Sex is not just a physical act; it is both psychological and physical. Studies have shown that sexual problems are more likely to occur because of psychological difficulties than a physical cause. This can occur whether or not the person has AS.

Psychological issues can trigger dysfunctions such as premature ejaculation, retarded ejaculation and impotence. If these problems are not discussed between the couple and help is not sought out, it is unlikely that they will be resolved on their own. Sexual problems can cause tremendous frustration and in the worst cases be responsible for the relationship breakdown. These problems can have a physical source, which should be checked out with a GP before looking at other causes. For the purpose of this section I am going to assume the reasons are psychological and not physical. If we take the three problem areas one by one we can look at the role AS might have in them.

Premature ejaculation quite simply means that the man reaches an orgasm before penetration or within a very short space of time afterwards, usually before the woman can receive any satisfaction from the act. It can cause disappointment for both and the woman can be left feeling used and unloved. She may feel her partner was being selfish or just wanted to satisfy himself, having no concern for her pleasure and whether or not she was satisfied. If this is not discussed with the man and he is unaware that it is causing a problem for her, it is unlikely that anything will change. One man I spoke to said he thought his wife just wanted to get it over and done with as quickly as possible, because she never gave him the impression she wanted him to continue for longer.

In order for a man to be able to control orgasm he has to be aware of what is going on with his body. He needs to be in touch with the physical sensations he is feeling; it requires that mind and body be linked. If he is anxious or worried about his performance, his mind will not be fully focused on the bodily sensations that lead him to orgasm.

Anxiety and AS are often linked together. The AS man is constantly having to work harder at reading situations and trying to work out if he is getting it right. The more he focuses on this the less he will be focusing on what his own body is doing. The more often he reaches an orgasm too quickly, the more anxious he will get about his performance. Once this pattern is fixed it can be extremely difficult to break.

One man with Asperger syndrome reported that he always seemed to fail at everything he did, and he always managed to upset his partner no matter how hard he tried not to. He and his wife had come to counselling and they were struggling very hard with the problems premature ejaculation was causing their relationship. It took many weeks work to change the thought patterns he had developed about his inadequacy. He never achieved the ability to delay orgasm for more than a few minutes, but he did learn that there were many other ways he could satisfy his partner. Once she felt more convinced that he was not just being selfish and did want to satisfy her, they could both work on rebuilding their sexual life and found that it improved considerably. The result was that they both felt happier and more satisfied physically and psychologically.

Retarded ejaculation is a difficulty in reaching an orgasm and can vary greatly in severity. The more severe it is the harder it is to put right. It is about too much control and holding back. For some men it only happens while they are having intercourse, and they may find it possible to reach an orgasm while having oral sex or being manually stimulated by their partner. Others may only be able to reach an orgasm through masturbation. Anxiety or inner conflict with the partner can cause retarded ejaculation. It can also be caused by anxiety over commitment issues with their partner; this type normally manifests itself in an inability to ejaculate inside the woman.

The man becomes anxious and in quite the opposite way to premature ejaculation, he focuses his anxieties on holding back and therefore prevents the voluntary physical action of ejaculation. He still experiences the pleasure of intercourse but does not ejaculate.

To overcome this, other areas of conflict in the couple relationship have to be investigated and resolved. The man then needs to focus on something else besides having an orgasm; he has to distract himself from thinking about ejaculation, maybe by thinking about something erotic.

Success in treating retarded ejaculation can depend quite strongly on what is actually causing it and also the man's willingness to discuss it openly. One man I saw with his partner had never ejaculated inside his wife; he had achieved it in a previous short-term relationship, but not with her. She said she felt unattractive and undesirable. He was initially unwilling to explore the reasons why he could not ejaculate inside his wife.

After many weeks of trust building and developing a better understanding of Asperger syndrome by both of them, the reasons behind this started to unfold.

His mother had been a very possessive and controlling woman. Sex was painted as very dirty and rarely discussed in the house. He had no sexual encounters in his teenage years and although he admits he was curious, he focused more on his academic pursuits than on looking for a sexual encounter. When he was just twenty he had a relationship with a girl in his tutor class at university. She was quite naive and came from a very strict Catholic upbringing that did not permit birth control. He was also quite naive and when they had sex he told her he would withdraw before ejaculation. Unfortunately he lost control and ejaculated before this could happen. His girlfriend was very upset and scared that she would become pregnant. Her worst nightmare became a reality, their parents had to be told and things really became quite nasty. The girl miscarried at fourteen weeks; she never did forgive him for letting her down. This was an awful and stressful time for him and he had linked ejaculation with the way it had made him feel. This link was very resilient and he developed some very strong barriers against ejaculating. It had almost become a rule to him that could not be broken, a boundary that could not be crossed.

Adults with Asperger syndrome often find it hard to put a situation into its appropriate context. Links made in earlier years can be carried through life if they are not recognized and challenged, and even then may be impossible to change.

Earlier I described the man who perceived anyone who wore a baseball cap on back to front as being untrustworthy and a threat. This was because of his previous encounter with a group of thugs wearing baseball caps. He had generalized the behaviour of young men who wore a baseball cap back to front based on this one particular instance; all he saw was the baseball cap, not the person wearing it.

Likewise, the young man had felt so upset by the anger and trauma that had occurred because he had lost control and ejaculated, that he applied it to all situations involving the same act. He did not recognize that the problem in his past was because the girl was young and the consequence of their lovemaking was an unwanted pregnancy. In order to avoid the uncomfortable feeling that reaching ejaculation now gave him he controlled it to the point where he became unable to ejaculate.

A problem from the past is only one of the reasons why retarded ejaculation occurs; there may be other issues behind it, especially if the man feels he is being pressured into having sex. It is though often linked to an incident that has happened in the past and it is necessary to explore, without pressure, what the initial trigger may have been.

Impotence, the inability to achieve an erection, was the problem most frequently mentioned by the couples I spoke to who were experiencing sexual problems. For some of these couples there had been a complete abstinence from sex for many years, sometimes decades. Most of these women felt cheated, undesirable and frustrated, and most did not have any idea why their partners could not make love to them. Some of the answers to why this happened came from the AS men I spoke to. Many of these men said that they preferred masturbation to making love with their partners. Asperger syndrome can result in the individual following very solitary pursuits, often having hobbies and interests that only involve themselves. Many adults with AS develop their own way of doing things and enjoy the control this gives them. It is far less complicated to do things alone than it is to involve someone else. It cuts out the difficulty involved in trying to understand and having to accommodate someone else's needs.

One man I spoke to was a keen cyclist. His wife tried very hard to join in and share this with him, but she had to do it his way, which meant cycling on his routes and at his speed. So, yes, he would let her share his interest with him but only if she allowed him, without argument, to take total control. This can also be applied in some cases to lovemaking; yes, he will make love but if she is not prepared to do it his way according to his timing and pace then he may decide he prefers to do it alone.

Masturbation in preference to shared lovemaking is not uncommon in cases of Asperger syndrome. This leads many women to believe that their partners are impotent and unable to make love. Often this is not the case and the man is able to achieve an erection and have an orgasm; he does not, however, want to achieve this in order to make love to her, he is happier and feeling more in control if he can masturbate instead.

Impotence may also develop for other reasons: maybe because he is angry with her over an unresolved issue. Adults with Asperger syndrome will often do anything they can to avoid confrontation, and if this means keeping quiet and not voicing what they are angry about, that is what they will do. This can result in impotence or a refusal to make love. It is his way of saying there is something he is not happy with or angry about. If this is not resolved early on and he begins to masturbate instead of having sexual intercourse, it could result in becoming a fixed routine, which once established will be very difficult to break.

Another problem in lovemaking that can lead to a refusal to make love can be caused by an over-sensitive reaction to sensory stimulation. This can show itself in many different ways. There may be an over-sensitivity to smell, touch or specific fabrics.

One couple had been experiencing sexual problems. When I asked them about this the man quickly told me that his partner complained that he was obsessive about being clean and he was aware that this was probably correct. His over-insistence on being scrupulously clean had for her been a complete turn off in bed and it was she who did not want to make love. She explained how they would get in bed together and he would lean over and ask if she had flossed her teeth. If she answered no, he would take this as 'No, I do not want sex with you tonight, and therefore I have not flossed my teeth.' If she had flossed her teeth then he would kiss her; he then might ask her when she had had a shower, or had she washed her hair today. If they did get as far as making love she was expected to jump straight out of bed afterwards and shower. He would not accept her just having a wash, it had to be a shower or bath, regardless of what time of night it was.

This became more and more a bone of contention between them. When he began to time sex by waiting until she got out of the bath or shower, regardless of what else she was about to do or whether she wanted sex at this time, it was the final straw. She started to refuse to have sex with him altogether, she said he made her feel like an object and did not accept her as a real flesh and blood human being.

Some men can be highly sensitive to touch and for one man I spoke to intercourse was actually painful, which caused many problems with his partner who could not understand why he jumped and flinched when they had sex. Other men have reported being over-sensitive in the nipple area, or on the arms or back. It helps for their partner to be aware of this so they can avoid these areas.

Particular fabrics may also be unpleasant to touch for the AS adult, and some will avoid contact with certain materials, but will not always tell their partner what it is that is causing them concern. One woman thought she would warm up the bed by putting on flannelette sheets, her husband was very restless and agitated throughout the night and finally got out of bed and slept on top of the duvet. He would not say what the problem was and his wife was left to figure it out. When she took off the flannelette sheets and replaced them with the usual cotton sheets everything went back to normal.

Sexual problems can occur in any relationship whether one of the partners has Asperger syndrome or not. They can be a lot harder to sort out and resolve though with the problems in communication caused by Asperger syndrome. The breakdown of the sexual side in any relationship is often a clear indication that there are problems elsewhere in the relationship and it is in danger of breaking down altogether. For some couples I spoke to, these issues had never been discussed or resolved. One AS man had turned to masturbation rather than having an affair, hence the issue was never pushed to a point where confrontation became inevitable and help was sought.

The majority of the AS women I spoke to seemed to divide into two different camps. Some did not appear to need sex in their relationships and the very idea was so distasteful that they almost cringed at the thought, while others expressed a very open attitude toward sex.

One woman I spoke to felt completely unable to make love with her partner, because she felt her partner and the whole sexual act to be messy and unclean. She did not view it as an emotional or loving act; it was purely a physical function that involved two bodies coming together. She was very aware of the clinical aspects and how these involved mingling of body fluids and body odours. Seeing making love purely from this point of view was repulsive to her and she had never allowed her partner to consummate the marriage. This was not felt to be an issue or problem between them, he found a release in masturbation and she said she had far more interesting pursuits to follow.

For others there was a very open attitude to sex and it was completely separated from emotion and seen as a means to an end. It gave them physical satisfaction; they found the act straightforward, uncomplicated and not requiring extensive mental effort. They just enjoyed sex for the pleasure it gave them, and for some of the women I spoke to this was not always exclusively with their partner.

Having Asperger syndrome does not automatically mean having sexual problems. Asperger syndrome causes problems in communication and social interaction and as sex is a form of communication, it is this that causes the problems, rather than the person's ability to have sex. It is not surprising that my research showed that it was reading the signs, responding to them and learning what the rules are that caused difficulties. Probably the most detrimental part that Asperger syndrome plays in the sexual relationship is that it can lessen AS adults' need to share the physical satisfaction that achieving an orgasm can bring them with a partner. Physical satisfaction can just as easily be achieved and enjoyed in solitude, very much like the other special interests or needs in the life of the person with Asperger syndrome.

Key points

- For some AS men sex is the easiest way for them to convey their feelings to their partner.
- Sometimes the AS man can become obsessive with getting his sexual performance perfect.
- It can be that the AS man finds it very difficult to initiate sex.
- The AS adult's difficulty in reading non-verbal signals can cause problems.
- Some AS men felt pressurized to perform, and uncomfortable with certain aspects of sex.
- Some AS men complain that sex is not frequent enough.
- A large proportion of AS couples do not have sex at all.
- Psychological issues can trigger sexual dysfunctions.

- Premature ejaculation and retarded ejaculation are about control.
- Impotence is frequently mentioned as a problem in the sexual relationship.
- Many AS men preferred masturbation to penetrative sex.
- The AS adult's sensitivity to touch can cause difficulties.
- AS women seem to divide into two camps in their views on sex. Some do not appear to need sex in their relationships, while others possess a very open attitude toward sex.

14

Infidelity

I have not encountered anyone with Asperger syndrome who had a hetero-sexual relationship with someone purely because they needed someone in their life just for sex. Sex was rarely the prime motivator for a relationship and this is probably the reason why infidelity in relationships where the man has Asperger syndrome is quite unusual but, as this chapter and the next one will show, not completely unheard of.

Seventy-five per cent of the men in my research had remained sexually faithful to their partners for all of the relationship, sometimes for many decades. This was one good aspect of the relationship that the women found gave them a lot of security. This faithfulness may be for many reasons. I asked one man why he had remained faithful to his wife even though they had not had sex for many years. He looked very surprised that I should be asking such a question and answered that his wife was a good mother and a good wife, she was a good cook and kept the house clean and ironed his shirts.

'Why would I want another woman?' he asked me.

Most men with AS seem to have a mental checklist on what they need from a partner and what qualities she has to have. Needing the woman to be sexual rarely gets a mention and when I looked at reasons why men with Asperger syndrome might be unfaithful, sex did not even come into the equation. Sex was certainly not a motive to have an affair with another woman, just as it was rarely the reason why the person with Asperger syndrome was attracted to his partner in the first place. Sex certainly seems to take a lower order in priority than is sometimes the case in NT relationships. It seems far more likely that if an AS man or woman had an affair it would be because the other person made them feel needed, liked or special and this need was not being met in his or her primary relationship. Finding someone else sexually attractive or desirable was never mentioned.

This is a pattern that probably begins in childhood. Children with Asperger syndrome can find it difficult to form friendships, during their schooldays, that last. They may have the desire to be popular and have lots of friends but, due to lack of social skills, they do not always manage to achieve this. One way AS children can be popular is through a special interest or because they might be particularly good at a specific sport or an area of learning. One teenage boy was excellent at science and found himself very popular when some difficult assignment was given to the class. He suddenly became in demand and felt quite needed and important. He was unable to see that this was because his friends needed his expertise and were not seeking him out because they liked him: they were not really friends.

This does not always change in adulthood and some adults with Asperger syndrome still feel the need to be liked and be popular. It may be that they are in a good position at work; it may be because they are very generous or gullible. If they feel liked or needed they will probably respond to this and not realize that they are heading into an affair and that they are possibly being used for more than just their companionship. It is very unlikely that the AS adult will initiate an affair or actually go looking for one, but if it is offered to them they may not always say no, particularly if they are feeling rejected or unwanted at home.

The effect of an AS adult's infidelity on his partner and family is just as devastating as it is in an NT relationship. The affair, though, is often for other reasons than to fulfil their sexual needs and some AS adults have had affairs that did not actually involve sex or at least not sexual intercourse.

One couple I spoke to had come to see me because of the husband's infidelity. Both were in their thirties and had been married only two years. She presented me with a telephone account that showed lists of numbers that her husband had contacted. Some she said were adverts from women looking for a relationship on the side; others were just to meet someone.

She had said he had met some of the women and one he had seen for a few weeks.

'How could you do this?' she asked. 'I trusted you so much to be faithful!'

'I have never been unfaithful to you!' he stated quite strongly.

She called him a liar and he was quite offended and threatened to leave the room.

I asked if he could be given time to justify what he was saying despite the evidence she had gathered against him. He agreed that he had contacted and met other women but still insisted that he had not done anything wrong. His wife was finding it very hard not to interject; she was very upset at his refusal to take any responsibility for what he had done.

'I was only doing what my wife had told me to do,' he said defensively.

At this point his wife was getting very annoyed. He said he would not discuss it in front of her any more and refused to say anything further on the subject. We agreed for the couple to not discuss it again until our next appointment.

The next time we met, we started by making some very clear agreements that anger would be controlled and space would be given to hear out what was being said. We began by sorting out what he meant when he said he had not done anything wrong, and when we talked about the meaning of infidelity he said that meant having sex with someone else. I asked him to define what sex was to him and he said sex to him meant having intercourse. As he had not had intercourse with anyone else he had not been unfaithful, so his wife was wrongly accusing him. He followed this by commenting that if it were not for his wife he would not have gone and met anyone in the first place. When I asked him what he meant by this comment he said his wife had told him to go and meet other women! I looked at his wife who at this instant I was afraid might not be able to hold to our agreement over anger control, but she did, although I could almost feel her growing frustration and rage.

I asked him to clarify what he meant. 'She told me she was sick of listening to me talk about motor racing and suggested that I find some other woman who would sit there listening to me going on and on. So I did!' he said. 'And I must say that they quite enjoyed hearing what I had to say.' The tension in the room instantly eased, his wife could remember quite clearly what she had said and even when she had said it. She explained to him that she did not mean for him to go out there and actually do it. He said he had not realized how upset she would be when she found out.

This couple worked out a compromise and decided to join a rally club that would enable him to talk about motor racing and her to make friends with the wives and partners who also came along.

It is very important for the NT woman to always be aware of what she is saying and whether her partner has taken it in the literal sense, which is not uncommon in Asperger syndrome. It is essential to clarify what the rules and boundaries are in a relationship and that both partners know what actions are defined as infidelities. Take for instance the word sex, what is sex and what is not sex? To the man in the scenario above, sex meant intercourse. He had confessed that one woman had kissed him and he had found it OK, but in his mind this was not being unfaithful because he did not have intercourse with her. The boundaries and rules of the relationship need to be discussed and clarified at the very beginning of the relationship; it is not enough take it for granted that the AS partner automatically knows exactly what the rules are.

Sometimes the interest in other women is because of an obsession with a particular aspect of a woman's anatomy. One man had an obsession with bottoms and would go out of his way to stand behind a woman who had a large bottom. He had no intention of doing anything but he caused a lot of embarrassing moments with his behaviour when it became obvious what he was looking at. Holidays used to be a nightmare and his partner had to tolerate him seeking out the woman with the biggest bottom on the beach to place his towel by. He could not see why it upset her so much and how she felt his attention to other women in this way was cruel and quite abusive. He actually wanted her to join in with his fixation and share the joy that big bottoms gave him. He could not see the pain and destruction he was causing to her and their relationship.

The attraction to another woman can be quite naive and innocent. It may be because she is in authority, powerful or has quite simply been nice to him. When the woman does not reciprocate his attention and he persists in displaying his attraction to her, it can become a problem if she sees it as stalking or sexual harassment. This can be especially problematic, and if the object of attraction is a young girl and his friendliness is misread as perverse and threatening, even though for him his intentions were not sexual and quite harmless, others might automatically presume he is a threat. He may have stood too close to her or given her mixed messages and all this could make a young person feel very intimidated.

Giving out mixed messages because of inappropriate eye contact or body language is not uncommon with Asperger syndrome. Eye contact can be quite evasive, but it can also be too constant, and eye contact held for too long can be seen as a sign of sexual attraction. Standing too close can also cause someone to feel threatened or harassed. All these actions can give off inappropriate and inaccurate signals and before long the AS man may find himself in trouble without knowing what he has done wrong.

A few women described their partners as being flirts and on more than one occasion have accused them of flirting with their friends, which has caused a lot of embarrassment for everyone. One reason for this is that just as adults with Asperger syndrome can give out the wrong signals, they can also read other people's signals incorrectly. They might confuse someone being friendly to them as a 'come on' or a sexual pass and then they may give out signals back to them that could appear flirtatious. This flirting can often be quite coy or boyish and although the person being flirted with might feel flattered, his behaviour will be quite infuriating for his partner. When questioned by their NT partners about the way they behaved most of the men said they were just talking or being friendly and accused their partners of being jealous or possessive. More often than not the AS man's intentions are not sexual and are really just about trying to be liked; he is not aware of how his actions and mannerisms might be interpreted by his partner.

So far I have written about men and infidelity. It is also an issue with women with Asperger syndrome. One-third of the AS women had had heterosexual relationships outside the marriage; one had had many sexual encounters with other men because she felt sorry for them. The men she chose were often much older than she and often disabled in some way. She did not feel she was committing adultery because she had no intention of leaving her husband. She said that as he was not disabled he did not need her like the other men did. She felt in some way empowered by being able to give the men something they wanted, and enjoyed their approval and the attention they gave her. The moral aspect of what she was doing and the risks she was taking had not occurred to her until she became involved with a man who became violent with her and this led to her husband discovering her affair.

When her husband asked her what had been going on, she simply told him the whole truth and in no way attempted to lie or deceive him. In this incident both the partners had Asperger syndrome, and although he only had traits of AS he had missed the signs that she was being unfaithful to him, he had presumed that she was faithful. They had not been having sex at the time so he had concluded that as she did not want sex with him she could not possibly want it with anyone else. When I asked her whether she had realized the pain and upset the deceit would cause her husband, she said 'No', because she had never lied to him. She justified her actions by saying that if he had asked her if she was having affairs with other men she would have told him, she said that he had never asked her so she presumed he just knew and it was OK.

This relationship is not representative of all cases of women with Asperger syndrome, and two-thirds of the sample of AS women had remained faithful. Whether a woman has extramarital relationships is dependent on many factors besides having AS. It may depend on the woman's sex drive, whether her needs are being met, the relationship the couple have and just how well the rules are discussed and laid down. The latter is essential when one or both partners have Asperger syndrome in a relationship.

There are also cases where the rules and boundaries may be carried over from a past relationship and new rules may not have been discussed and negotiated. It can be very easy for the NT partner to presume the AS partner automatically knows what these rules are. All too often these presumptions are wrong and the rules and boundaries need to be firmly understood and established. Despite these problems I found that seventy-five per cent of the couples I had come into contact with were monogamous; the majority of the AS men and women had remained faithful to their partners.

In some of the cases of infidelity it was not the AS partner who had been unfaithful, it was the NT partner who had had an affair, and this had caused some very extreme reactions in the partner with Asperger syndrome. One man I interviewed had discovered by accident that his wife was having an affair with a colleague at work. He had not expressed his anger directly to her but had made it his mission in life to discover who this person was. The extremes he went to were quite phenomenal and alarming.

Unknown to his wife he booked two weeks leave from work. He pretended to still go to work but by a slow and drawn-out process of elimination he eventually pinpointed the man he thought his wife was having an affair with. He followed them and took notes and photographs as he compiled his evidence against her. He soon discovered this man's name and address and, when he knew that the man would be at work, he went around to see the man's wife. He informed the wife of what had been happening, giving her the dates and times of the affair. As a consequence the other man's marriage broke down.

He then challenged his wife with the evidence and made threats to take the children from her. He stayed with his wife for another two years before he drove her away with his cruel comments, constant digs and reminders of what she had done. He made her suffer relentlessly for the affair and when I spoke with him, over ten years later, he was still bitter and still kept tags on his ex-wife just to make sure she never got together with this man. It did not concern him if she had a relationship with anyone else, but the man she had the affair with was still the focus of bitter and very deep resentment.

It is unlikely that if trust is lost in this way the adult with Asperger syndrome will ever give his partner his trust again and actually recover enough for the relationship to continue. Even if there are significant reasons why the affair happened in the first place, it is unlikely he will see any justification for the betrayal. The AS adult may be totally unwilling to see that he may have played a part in what went wrong and that he may have neglected his partner's and the relationship's needs. He will be blind to the fact that the affair may have been a consequence of something he was doing or not doing. His focus will be on the affair and everything that goes wrong in the future or had gone wrong in the past may be blamed on it.

However, unfaithfulness was present in only a minority of the couples I interviewed. In the few relationships where infidelity had occurred, some had survived and some had not. What was interesting was that in four of the relationships that had involved the partner with Asperger syndrome being unfaithful, the person they were unfaithful with was the same sex as they were. This will be discussed in the next chapter.

Key points

- ○ Most AS men remain faithful to their partners.
- ○ Sex seems to take a relatively low priority in AS relationships.
- ○ Definitions of what equates to infidelity need to be decided between the couple.
- ○ Some AS men may become interested in other women because of an obsession with a particulat aspect of a woman's body.
- ○ AS men can find themselves being accused of flirtatious behaviour because of their failure to read non-verbal signs.
- ○ Most AS women are faithful to their partners.
- ○ It has been known for an AS man to go to extreme lengths because he suspected his partner of having an affair.

15

Sexuality and Asperger Syndrome

Sexuality and Asperger syndrome is a very understudied area. Three of the men and one woman I spoke to had had a relationship with a same sex partner. I have not yet come into contact with any man or woman with Asperger syndrome who stated he or she was exclusively homosexual or lesbian. This is not to say that absolute homosexuality does not occur in the Asperger population, as having Asperger syndrome does not determine sexual preference. It is more likely that I just have not been contacted by anyone in this situation.

Until this point, my research had shown me that AS men rarely have an affair purely for sexual reasons. The scenario, however, was not the same for the men in my research who had homosexual affairs; these relationships were primarily of a sexual nature.

All of the NT women whose AS partner had been involved in homosexual relationships were aware of their partners' sexual practices and these practices had become accepted by them. They had no sexual contact with their partners. The AS men who had had affairs with other men had done so purely from a sexual angle and not because of any emotional involvement. The AS men found the sexual arrangement they had had with other men far more tolerable and less stressful than trying to meet the emotional demands placed upon them by their wives. A woman may be more likely to regard sex as a very emotional experience and expect a level of reciprocation from her partner. This may further explain why in half of the heterosexual relationships there was no sexual activity.

Showing and displaying emotions can be difficult for the man with AS. If too many emotional demands are made during the sexual act he may stop having sex with his partner altogether and while some turn to masturbation, three men in my research formed sexual relationships with other men.

None of these AS men made any reference to being attracted to other men or finding them physically desirable. They did not want to spend time with them outside the sexual relationship and did not want to live with them. So whether these relationships were a convenient way of escaping frustration is subject to conjecture. The men who had these relationships also felt that they had not really been unfaithful to their wives, as the sexual partner was a man rather than another woman. They did not feel the homosexual relationship had changed their sexuality in any way and still regarded themselves as heterosexual men. This is in part due to the fixed identity of self that is often established early in AS men, there is often a reluctance to change the conventional label of heterosexuality. The AS person wants to be perceived as 'normal' as possible in the eyes of society, falling in line with society's edicts. He may feel that a bisexual label would compromise this perception of him. Because the homosexual relationships formed by these men appear to be unemotional acts with no form of commitment, they do not appear of significant enough to cause any change to their self-identity.

The AS woman who had been involved in a lesbian relationship said that the feelings she had for the other woman were sexual and emotional. She said that she found this particular woman very attractive. The AS woman was married and cared about her husband, but did not have a sexual relationship with him as he had a long-term illness that precluded him from having sex. His wife did not regard her lesbian relationship as being unfaithful.

The lesbian affair had been long-term and the AS woman reported that she had a strong attachment to her girlfriend, especially as they enjoyed sharing the same interest together. I asked if her husband knew.

'Oh no, he would be very upset if he knew. He thinks homosexuality is perverse!'

I asked if she felt any guilt about what she was doing.

'No,' she replied, 'I have never lied to my husband and never would.'

I then asked whether she considered what she was doing deceitful.

'No,' she said. 'I have never deceived him, he has never asked me whether I am having sex with my friend.'

This woman's interpretation was that she had not broken any rules in the relationship, had not lied, deceived or been unfaithful. This was her perception and she defended it passionately.

Asperger syndrome does not determine sexuality; it may though affect the way the affairs of the men were carried out in such an unemotional and objective manner. The affairs served a purpose and are not allowed in any way to encroach on the primary relationship. The affairs are viewed as sexual and practical, rather than fulfilling any emotional need.

Transvestism or cross-dressing is not about being homosexual, although it can occur in homosexual relationships. It is when a man dresses in women's clothes either because it makes him feel relaxed or because he gains sexual excitement from it. It may be that the man finds the pressures of being male stressful and if he wears women's clothes it can take away the responsibility that being a man can bring. It can also be a very tactile practice, for example, the feel of silk stockings or underwear can be sexually stimulating. Male cross-dressing often starts in boyhood, maybe as an experiment, a young boy dresses up in his mother's or sister's underwear and then masturbates. If he reaches an orgasm, he may link the pleasure this sensation gave him to the clothes he is wearing. Cross-dressing can quickly become an essential part of the masturbation process as the clothes increase his arousal level. It is an extremely difficult cycle to break once it has become established. The cross-dresser may go through periods when he will get rid of all the clothes and not cross-dress for quite a long time. However, during times of stress, it may manifest itself again.

I have encountered two cases of cross-dressing in AS men. One was based purely on the sensation that silk gave the cross-dresser when worn next to his body. At times, he wore his wife's underwear under his trousers as he found it relaxing. The other man I spoke to took cross-dressing much further. He was not in a relationship at the time so had the freedom to cross-dress whenever he pleased. His cross-dressing though did cause him some problems. On one occasion when he came to see me, I got the impression that he was very despondent and depressed. I asked him the reason for this. He told me he had come to the conclusion that he was not very convincing when dressed as a woman.

He said he had gone for a drive in the car while cross-dressed. He drove a lot a further than he had intended and realized he was quite hungry. He was driving through a popular tourist town and decided he would stop and get something to eat in one of the many restaurants. He had believed that his dress was so convincing that he would be accepted as female. As luck would have it, he had parked and was locking his car at exactly the same time a pack of bikers were riding by. He felt uneasy but thought that they would not realize he was a man and he would get away with it. Unfortunately, they saw through his subterfuge instantly and he was the target of much verbal abuse and jeering. He got back in his car very quickly, locked himself in and drove off. They gave chase, only for a short distance, but he was very scared by the whole episode. He did not call the police because he did not want to be discovered dressed as a woman.

When I asked him why he took such a risk, he said it had not occurred to him that they would think he was a man. Some men can be quite convincing when they cross-dress, but this man was 6' 4" tall and took size thirteen shoes. He was a very large-built man and would never have physically been able to pass as a woman. Because in his mind he felt like a woman when he cross-dressed, he presumed that everyone else would see him as he perceived himself. The incident could have been worse but it had shaken him up. He realized after this that he could not pass as a woman; he blamed it on the fact that his shoes were men's, as he could not find any women's shoes in a size thirteen.

One area of uncharted territory is the area of male or female prostitution and Asperger syndrome. I have not come across any women who have received money for sex, but did encounter an AS man in his early twenties who had built up a relationship with an older male which had continued for many years. It never went beyond mutual masturbation and was seen purely as a means to an end, i.e. sexual gratification. The man concerned did not view himself as participating in prostitution and viewed it purely as an arrangement between himself and his contact. There had been no other relationships with men, but he said he would have other liaisons if he was offered payment and if he liked the man or woman involved. His other relationships had only ever been with women and he said he intended to marry and have children at some point in the future.

I do not feel that there is any correlation between Aspergers syndrome and cross-dressing, homosexuality, sexual deviancies, fetishes or prostitution and would say issues regarding sexuality are likely to occur in an individual regardless of whether he or she has Asperger syndrome or not. What is different is probably how the behaviour is perceived and interpreted by the person concerned and the reasons it happens in the first place. None of the adults with Asperger syndrome who had had sexual relationships outside the primary relationship showed any sign of guilt, remorse or concern for what they had done, and viewed it with an objective attitude.

So does this lack of guilt and remorse display itself in other aspects of the life of someone with Asperger syndrome? Next we look at verbal abuse and domestic violence.

Key points

- Most AS men who have homosexual affairs do so purely from a sexual angle.
- Most AS men do not feel the homosexual relationship changed their sexuality.
- An AS woman who had a lesbian affair does not perceive herself as being unfaithful.
- Cross-dressing in AS can be about the texture and feel of fabrics.
- Lack of awareness and cross-dressing can have a potentially dangerous side for the AS man.
- For one AS man, receiving money for sexual favours is purely a means to an end.
- There are no known links between sexuality, cross-dressing or prostitution and having Asperger syndrome.

16

Verbal Abuse and Asperger Syndrome

About seventy per cent of the AS men answered 'Yes' to the question, 'Had they ever been verbally abusive to their partners?' Forty per cent of these quickly justified their answer with an excuse or reason as to why they had been verbally abusive. Many argued it was in retaliation to their partner's verbal abuse.

The most extreme case of verbal abuse came from a woman with Asperger syndrome who openly admitted to being very abusive towards her husband. She stated quite firmly that she really did not like him very much and was quite open and honest in saying so. She actively looked forward to his death so he would not be around to annoy her any more and she could live alone. Her husband had also been diagnosed with Asperger syndrome and his obsessive behaviour was so strong that he had also been diagnosed with obsessive-compulsive disorder. One of his obsessions was that he felt compelled to listen to the daily news broadcasts. It did not matter whether it was via the television or radio, as long as he got to hear the news, whenever possible. Either the television or the radio would be on constantly; to him it was vital that he listened to it and he felt very threatened and anxious if he missed the latest news broadcast. This would raise his stress level and he would become very withdrawn and depressed.

His wife was the complete opposite, she liked peace and quiet and found the constant noise of the radio or TV to be very frustrating, inhibiting her ability to concentrate on anything else. The noise affected her like chalk on a blackboard and she would cover her ears and scream if he would not turn it off. She would try to cope for a while and then when she had overstretched her tolerance level she would suddenly erupt in a fit of temper, displaying very typical Asperger anger. She would call him all the derogatory names that came into her head. When this happened he would jump up, turn the radio or television off and leave the room as quickly as possible. Her outburst would last for about sixty seconds and then stop as abruptly as it had started, afterwards she would just carry on as though the incident had not happened.

I suggested to this couple that he purchase some earphones for his radio so when she was around he could plug his earphones in and listen to the news without disturbing her. He did, and it did help the situation. There were still episodes when she would become angry and call him names, but now he is able to turn up the sound and not hear her.

AS anger can be very unpredictable and irrational. It can appear completely out of context, take all those around by total surprise and leave everyone in a state of bewilderment as to what they had said or done to provoke such an outburst. Just as quickly as it starts, it may stop, and the AS person will just want everything to return to normal and be quite surprised if his partner is upset and unable to forget about it. For the NT partner the damage and destruction caused by the outburst cannot be forgotten, and he or she may want to retaliate; the arguments and verbal abuse were quite severe in some of the relationships. Many times this total breakdown in the relationship could have been avoided if each partner had been able to understand the other's perception. Verbal abuse often begins at the point where communication on an acceptable level breaks down and the partners feel misunderstood and not heard.

One man had told his wife he was going to get fuel for his car as he did not want to bother getting it in the morning when the traffic and queues were bad. She was getting dinner ready at the time, so she just nodded and asked could he get a bottle of their favourite red wine while he was out. 'OK', he said and left. Time passed, she kept turning off the dinner and warming it up again thinking any minute he would walk in. Dinner soon spoiled and after waiting an hour and a half she was starting to get very concerned. He came home, looked around for his dinner and then spotted his wife standing by the cooker.

'Where have you been?' she shouted. 'Your dinner has completely spoilt, I have been worried to death, you have ruined everything again!'

The last part was all he heard and he saw this as another attack. He instantly became verbally aggressive, shouted and told her she was always attacking him, she was a nasty angry woman and in his opinion she was mentally disturbed and needed putting away. With this he threw his dinner in the bin and walked out. Afterwards he felt no remorse and felt his actions were justified as he had been out trying to get her the wine she wanted because, he said, she had moaned at him last time for getting the wrong one. He did not see how hard she had worked at cooking his dinner; even though he knew it was almost ready when he left, his entire focus had been on finding this particular wine. He had thought about nothing else, had not heard his wife saying she was worried about him, only hear her condemning him for trying to do his best.

Many AS men described how they felt attacked and criticized by their partners. Talking to their partners though showed this was not always the case and sometimes their partner said they were just highlighting something their husbands had done which had upset or hurt them. The AS partner would instantly interpret this as criticism, believe that she was verbally attacking him and retaliate by being abusive to her. This type of situation is all too familiar in Asperger relationships and is all the consequence of communication difficulties. Not all AS men react with verbal abuse; some will react with silence and withdrawal, which can be equally damaging for their partners.

Most AS men stated perceived criticism was the main reason for verbally abusing their partners. Although this was the major reason, it was not the only reason given. Some AS men felt that they were only verbally abusive in retaliation to their partner's verbal abuse. Many believed their partner pushed them into this deliberately. Only one AS man admitted that he was verbally abusive on purpose to try to gain control over his wife.

All the accounts given by NT partners showed that they felt very damaged by the verbal abuse thrown at them, but for some it was the silent and passive aggression that they felt was even more damaging. Many felt unheard and shut out by the silence and atmosphere of disapproval that could be directed at them by their AS partners. Silence can feel as abusive and damaging as verbal abuse. One only has to try not talking to and ignoring a child to see the affect it can have. Silence and being ignored can cause stress and anxiety. The uncertainty of not knowing what the other person is thinking can make the other partner feel rejected and insecure. It has been verbalized by some NT women that at least if he shouts and argues they know what is in his thoughts and how they should respond to it. Silence is different and it is a very powerful weapon when used in relationships. It can be used for different reasons, to gain attention, cause concern or to punish.

Some AS men have great difficulty dealing with aggression and confrontation, they may find it difficult to hold their position and argue back. Therefore they retreat, go silent and put up walls. They will do whatever it takes to help them cope with the anger and shouting directed at them. This does not mean that the silent person is any less angry than the person who makes a lot of noise and is verbally abusive, it probably means they are even angrier. The anger is contained; it is controlled and vented back in a very passive way. The AS partner may show his anger by not being affectionate, by not coming home or by being very critical of his partner, the children or her family, whichever hurts most.

One man paid his wife back by asking his secretary out for a drink. His secretary was young and attractive and he knew his wife was worried about having gained weight. Following an argument in which he had felt very criticized and put down, he suggested quite cuttingly that she have a chat with his secretary and ask how she kept her figure so trim. This really hurt his wife and when she discovered that he had gone out for a drink with his secretary she was devastated. She confronted her husband who said he had not thought she would mind, as all she seemed to do was shout at him lately. He had not made any attempt to hide the fact he had been out with his secretary as he had the date in his diary on the home computer. As he and his wife shared the computer it was inevitable that his wife would discover it.

It was his way of paying her back for the way he felt she had treated him. He knew that this would upset her, because his wife confided to him that she felt threatened by some of the women who worked for him. She had often said to him that she would be very hurt if he ever went out with one of them. This was his way of venting his anger towards her in a non-confrontational way. He maintained that he had not done anything he should be ashamed of, as the drink was business and they had only talked about work. His wife felt very shaken by what had happened and her confidence took quite a knock. He had gained control over their relationship and for him that was vital, as it appears to be for many adults with Asperger syndrome. Having Asperger syndrome and losing control can have some very threatening and damaging consequences for a relationship.

Key points

- The majority of AS men say they have been verbally abusive to their partners.
- Some of the AS men argued that they were verbally abusive to their partner only in retaliation to her verbal abuse.
- The most extreme case of verbal abuse was by an AS woman.
- AS anger can be highly explosive.
- Misunderstandings between the AS and NT partners are responsible for most cases of verbal abuse.
- NT women feel damaged by their partner's verbal abuse towards them.
- Some AS men use verbal abuse as a way of preventing their partner from confronting them.
- Some AS men use silence or cutting remarks as a way of retaliating.

17

Domestic Violence and Asperger Syndrome

Forty per cent of AS men in my research said that, at some time in their relationship, they had been physically abusive towards their partner. These figures are fairly high and might suggest that men with Aspergers have a tendency to be violent. However, drawing conclusions from the data in this area is far more complex than might first be apparent.

Whilst forty per cent is an alarmingly high figure, only ten per cent of these attacks were described as unprovoked. Statements like 'only in retaliation', 'only to restrain her' or 'only in response to extreme physical aggression' were used by the AS men who answered in the affirmative to this question. There may be an argument that these AS men are simply in denial or not taking responsibility for their physical aggression. However, in most of the examples, this was not the case, as their NT partners confirm that they did indeed attack them first, or that they were aware that their partners had to restrain them.

Although any type of violence in a relationship is unacceptable, the violence that was reported in my research was, in most cases, not extreme and rarely involved physical violence such as hitting, punching or kicking. For the greater part, it was described as pushing, shoving or restraining. Severe violence by AS men appeared to be less common but was reported in two cases and this involved hitting, throwing a partner against a wall and banging her head against a wall. These are all very serious acts of violence and should not be tolerated by the NT partner.

Most of the cases reported to me by the couples stated that violence had only occurred once or had been very infrequent. There were no reported cases of long term or chronic violence, and one of the two men who had been violent without provocation expressed remorse that he had hurt his partner. Forty per cent is still a high incidence of violence to be reported in a sample of this size and does suggest that this might be linked to the pressures that living in an Asperger relationship, often receiving very little support, can have. The reason why this happens is, at this stage, unknown, but could conceivably be attributed to the underlying dynamics of the individual relationship.

Reviewing the reasons that many NT women gave as to why they were attracted to their partners in the first place, it can be seen that they considered them to be gentle, quiet and kind men. The women were drawn to their submissive, quiet ways and appreciated their lack of aggression and dominance. Some of the NT women that I have been in dialogue with had at sometimes in their lives endured some form of abuse. For some, this was due to a dysfunctional upbringing and for others, a previous partner who was abusive. These women had been the victims of circumstances that were out of their control. Most had been emotionally abused and some physically and sexually abused as well. When they met their partners, they recalled how comfortable and safe they felt with these quiet non-aggressive men. Their new partners did not over-react or talk down to them or raise their voices. All this made them feel validated, worthy and very safe; they felt that they were in control.

In the course of time though, it is sometimes the traits that attract one person to another that become the very thing that begin to drive them apart. A woman may later realize that her AS partner does not show any emotional response towards her and she may interpret this as not caring and may find herself frustrated by his lack of response to her feelings. This frustration may also cause her to become physically aggressive in an attempt to provoke an emotional reaction from him. This may be why thirty per cent of the men reported that it was their partner who was physically abusive or threatening towards them. Maybe for some NT women, when words alone did not seem to have an affect, frustration and desperation for a reaction resulted in them being physically aggressive towards him. For most of the women who feel pushed into this role, it is not a natural role for them and it is a clear sign that they, their partner and the relationship desperately need help.

The fundamental issue is that domestic violence is about control and issues about control seem to be paramount in Asperger relationships whether it is verbal, physical or silent passive control. How severe this need for control is can depend on a number of factors, one of which is the personality of each partner. Some couples will be able to circumvent these problems through dialogue, for others the relationship will become a power struggle over who will have the most control.

One of the reasons why people with or without Asperger syndrome need control in a relationship is because of deep-rooted insecurities carried over from the past. For the NT women who have been the victims of abuse in the past, some form of control is often essential for them to have a level of security. An AS man may be quiet and non-demonstrative and may appear distant and have difficulty in giving up his autonomy. The feeling this can give his NT partner may be one of insecurity and loneliness, especially if she does not understand why he is behaving like this because she does not have an understanding of Asperger syndrome. These insecure feelings may increase her need for control, the more she tries to control him and get an emotional response the more distant he will become. If this is not rectified, it can result in a vicious cycle that is difficult to break. Physical abuse can be a consequence of these feelings of frustration.

AS men require control for different reasons; one is that it is essential and vital for them to maintain an order in their lives. Control is a fundamental necessity that allows them to exist in a confusing and complex neuro-typical world. Unfortunately, this can be at the expense of the NT partner and the control that is exerted on her can become extreme and irrational. It is at the point when the AS partner feels that he is loosing control that profound and illogical anger might unexpectedly be directed at his partner. Witnessing Asperger anger can be very frightening and intimidating. When anxiety reaches breaking point, the AS man may lose control of his feelings. He may suddenly erupt and lash out at the nearest object and make for the nearest exit. In desperation, the NT partner may try to block his retreat, this is when he may react physically and aggressively towards her if she does not move out of his way or let him go.

Although having AS in a relationship may play a part in physical abuse it is certainly not the only variable that causes a violent relationship. One of the reasons (not excuses) that determine whether or not a person is likely to be violent is his family upbringing. If a person is brought up in a violent household, it is likely that he may be familiar with a pattern of violence and this could result in a person becoming an instrument of violence or a victim of violence. This applies to all humankind, irrespective of whether they have Asperger syndrome or not. If the AS partner was brought up in a household that was functional and caring, it is less likely that he will be physically abusive towards his partner. If AS men grow up in a household that holds on to the rule that men do not hit women, and this rule is quite strongly enforced, then it is likely this edict will be respected in adult life.

Fortunately, the majority of the relationships in my research did not reach a violent state and those that did rarely involved severe cases of violence. But any form of physical abuse in a relationship is unhealthy for all concerned and when a person feels he is pushed by desperation into an abusive role his feelings of self-worth are reduced dramatically.

Many NT women said that, despite the fact that their partners had never harmed them, they still felt threatened. Some said that they felt there was a darker and more sinister side to their partners that at times made them feel quite fearful and wary. One woman who came to see me said she felt her life was in danger. I asked her why she felt like this as I knew her husband personally and he appeared to be a quiet placid man. She said that it was the way he looked at her. Their marriage had reached crunch point and she was in the process of divorcing him for unreasonable behaviour based on his obsessive need for routine and lack of responsibility in the marriage. He refused to accept that the marriage was over and chose not to hear her saying that she had had enough and wanted out. He would listen to what she said, walk away, come back and act as though things were just fine; it was as if she had not spoken. He just denied completely what she was saying to him. This had continued for many months; he would not sign the divorce petition and had made it as difficult as possible for her to break free of him. I asked her why she felt in fear of her life, and she said that someone had tampered with her car. This had happened on a few occasions and she thought it might be him. She had been to the police, and they had warned him, but she had no definitive evidence that he was responsible. I asked her why she thought it was her husband? The answer was that she did not know for sure – it was something in the way he looked at her.

Women ending relationships with AS partners have reported that they have been stalked or intimidated and made to feel very scared. In such cases, the behaviour of the AS partner is not acceptable and should not be sanctioned by these women or those in authority. In some incidences though, the AS partner's behaviour may not be as threatening as it appears. AS adults find change extremely hard to cope with, and when they are faced with a divorce or separation that is against their wishes, they can become extremely difficult to deal with. They still have the need to be part of their partner's lives, and breaking away is very hard for them. This could be seen as intimidating, but at times, they are still doing what they consider best for their partners or the children if there are any.

Very often, although the AS man's actions will appear intimidating and premeditated, he is just reacting to a situation and has not put any prior thought into it at all. One woman described how, after she and her husband had separated, he bought their son the latest Playstation and some very expensive games, but he would not let his son take them home and said he could only play with them when he came to see him. His wife could not compete with the expensive Playstation games and felt very angry; she said he was trying to buy her son's affection and control them both by what he was doing. Her husband's perspective was very different. He said he was afraid his son would not want to see him and thought if he bought him something he really liked, he would want to go round and see him, now that he had moved out. He said that he felt he did not know how to interact with his son and was uneasy trying to converse with him. A Playstation made it easier for him and was the only thing he felt he could offer his son as an incentive to go round. This man's actions had not been vindictive and he could not see that what he was doing was in any way controlling; he was unable to see his wife's perspective on this and felt he was the victim because his wife had such a good relationship with their son.

I also looked at violence in relationships when the woman had AS and this showed that an alarming seventy-five per cent of the women I spoke to had been physically abusive to their partners. In all of the cases, the violence involved hitting, punching or kicking. In one case the violence committed was quite extreme and long-term.

There may be various reasons for this; it may simply be due to the particular women who took part in this research. Not all of the AS women I spoke to were physically abusive towards their partners. It is difficult to be sure whether this high level of physical abuse is a consequence of the women having Asperger syndrome or more to do with these particular women being physically volatile. One reason for AS women being more susceptible to physically abusing their partners may be due to the social pressures that are placed on women in general, and society's expectation that women should conform to be good wives and good mothers. Society is far more shocked if a female attacks or harms someone than if a man does. Society is also more shocked when it hears of a mother causing harm to her partner or her children than when the abusive partner is male.

Women are still expected in many societies to be carers, nurturers and the passive ones in the family. A woman is often expected to put her whole family before herself and look after her family's needs and requirements before her own. She is also expected to do this by intuitiveness – instinctively knowing what those needs are. This can be a difficult task for most women but is particularly onerous for women with Asperger syndrome. This puts AS women under immense strain and the stress and the frustration this causes is likely to be one of the catalysts for the strong temper outbursts which are sometimes displayed by AS women. I have included more about this in Chapter 22 Women and Asperger Syndrome.

Another area of this research into abuse has been the differences that being aware of having Asperger syndrome can have on a relationship. I found that if the person with Asperger syndrome was unaware of its presence, or worse still, denied totally that he was affected by it, the chances of abuse increased dramatically. If he believed that the only person with a problem was his partner and blamed her, then the reported incidence of verbal and domestic violence towards her increased even more. This is discussed in the next chapter.

Key points

- Many AS men say that at some time they have been physically abusive towards their partners.

- Some AS men say that their physical abuse was in retaliation or to restrain their partners' attack on them.

- One AS woman and two AS men reported incidences of severe or chronic violence against their partners.

- Upbringing may affect any person's potential to be violent.

- Some NT women feel threatened by their partners although they have never harmed them.

- Ending a relationship and the process of divorce can be a potentially threatening time for the NT partner.

- There are reported cases of stalking and intimidation by AS partners.

- It is not always the AS person's intention to be intimidating or manipulating.

- A majority of AS women are at some time physically abusive towards their partners.

- More pressure may be put on AS women than on AS men in relationships.

- Incidence of violence within a relationship increases where AS is not acknowledged or accepted.

18

Asperger Syndrome and Awareness

It is often due to the diagnosis of a child that parents first learn about Asperger syndrome. It is also at this time that it may be recognized in one of the child's parents. There are times when this recognition comes as a relief as it brings with it an explanation of the problems and difficulties that the family are likely to have been experiencing. Sometimes it may come as a complete shock and be met with total denial. Some AS men never accept they have Asperger syndrome and although they may be very aware that there is a differential between the two partners in the relationship, they may lay the whole blame in their partners' laps.

One man insisted his wife was completely useless at communicating, despite the fact that she was a lawyer whose clients depended on her ability to communicate, convince and negotiate. At times he would become very verbally aggressive and physically threatening towards her. His stress levels would reach desperate heights, trying to get her to agree that the communication problems they were experiencing were her fault and that she was no good at communicating. She would not back down and the marriage eventually ended when he hit her. This man had not been diagnosed as having Asperger syndrome, but his son and cousin had. He had many traits that suggested strongly that he was on the autistic spectrum and his wife was quite convinced that he had AS.

Prior to the discovery that their son had Asperger syndrome they had been having marital problems. They had been to counselling three times and each attempt had failed miserably, leaving the relationship in a worse state than before. It was his wife's persistence that the behavioural pattern of her son was so similar to her husband's that led to the discovery that he had AS. As the couple learnt more and more about their son's condition, they both began to recognize that the father had the same traits as his son. Oddly enough he was the first to suggest that he was concerned he had Asperger syndrome, but then became very distraught and angry at the thought that this might be the case. Every time his wife spoke about their son, he would say, 'What are you trying to suggest, that I have AS too!' Talking about their son's condition became harder and harder for her and the distance between husband and wife, father and son grew. Her husband reacted to any form of perceived criticism with anger. He would accuse her of trying to make out he was a freak, at other times he would hold up his hands in despair and say, 'OK, OK you have got your own way, I am a freak, I can't communicate, I must have this Asperger thing!'

The situation went from bad to worse; his wife could do nothing to improve it. Then one day her husband announced that his son did not have Asperger syndrome and neither did he, the experts had got it wrong, his son was just a bit quiet and that was his mother's fault because she could not communicate properly. It became a clear case of 'shoot the messenger', and she was in his eyes the messenger. This woman came close to having a nervous breakdown, she felt frantic and desperate. She loved her husband very much but could not find any way to prevent his destructive and abusive behaviour. Things reached crunch point when he tried to prevent his son getting the extra help offered at school; they had a bitter row and he lost control, lashed out and hit her. That was when she decided enough was enough and that she had a responsibility to both herself and their son. She left because she felt that had she stayed both of them might be in danger. This was when she first came to see me; she was quite broken and desperate. The damage to her self-esteem and confidence took a long time to repair. Her husband stayed in denial and refused any help or advice, consequently both suffered a very bitter divorce.

In cases like this when the man denies he has Asperger syndrome, verbal abuse, domestic violence and other problems will increase within the relationship. The fact that AS is present will have caused difficulties in the relationship anyway. If he is in denial that the problems have anything to do with him and says they are his partner's fault, he will hear everything she says as criticism and she will get the blame for the problems they are having.

My research showed that if the couple accepts Asperger syndrome as being part of the problem and endeavours to increase their understanding of the disorder then many relationships actually improve. Discovery of the syndrome becomes the turning point in the relationship as it brings with it answers to many questions and offers a reason for many of the troubles the couples were likely to have been struggling with. Many of the AS men I spoke to felt a sense of relief and some described discovering Asperger syndrome as a revelation. Many had struggled for years with relationships and had not been able to understand why they kept getting it wrong, despite trying so hard to get it right.

One man described how he had always felt there seemed to be something his wife wanted of him, yet he could never figure out what it was. Another man said he did not have a clue what he was doing wrong, he just knew he always did. An AS man will be very aware of what his partner is saying to him. He hears her saying that he does not understand her, that he does not support her emotionally, and he may often interpret this as her saying he is useless and inadequate. When he realizes he has Asperger syndrome and understands what the disorder is about, he will also learn that many of the problems he has been having are caused by it. He will discover it was not all his fault; he has a peg to hang the problems on and can separate them from himself.

After the discovery of AS some men work harder at the relationship and are willing to listen to their partners and be guided by what they say. With the appropriate help and support the relationship can improve and all the family will benefit.

But what if he does not accept that he has Asperger syndrome? This is when the relationship will become especially problematic and often break down completely. Some AS men in relationships will not accept that there is a problem. I have found that the more severe the effects of Asperger syndrome are, the more likely this is to occur. This is not the case when the adult is so severely affected that they are unable to form and maintain a relationship. Rather it seems to be when the AS adult is somewhere in the middle, not so badly affected that they cannot form an intimate relationship, but affected badly enough for it to cause an almost total inability to empathize and an even more heightened sensitivity to criticism. This theory is based on my research and observation, it is not a proven fact, but it is certainly an area that could merit investigation.

I have found that although Asperger syndrome will disable the individual in the three core areas definied by diagnostic criteria, the degree to which these three areas are affected can vary dramatically between individuals. Perhaps awareness and acceptance of the syndrome is dependent on which of the three areas, communication, social interaction or imagination, are affected most. How the individual reacts towards perceived criticism seems to have a major effect on whether a diagnosis of Asperger syndrome is accepted. If he sees having AS means he is abnormal or unacceptable he will struggle with the label. If he feels it completely changes his self-identity and he will become a 'person with Asperger syndrome' then once again he may have difficulty coming to terms with the idea. In either case he may then begin to blame his partner, and if there is a heightened sensitivity to criticism it will be difficult for him to distinguish between positive and negative criticism and, in some cases, understand that caring and support can accompany the criticism.

During my initial research I looked at three different groups, each of ten or more couples. I asked the NT partners various questions about their relationships with their AS partners. Their replies were very interesting and when the different groups were compared each group said something quite different. It does though need to be remembered that this is based on the perception of the NT partner and the perception of the AS partner might have been quite different. This does not imply that the information I received was not honest, as it was very honest in the perception of the person supplying it.

Group A consisted of ten NT women whose partners had received a diagnosis of Asperger syndrome and both accepted the condition. Most of these couples had children and some of the children had also received a diagnosis for Asperger syndrome.

Group B consisted of twelve NT women whose children had received a diagnosis and the women were aware that their partners also had Asperger syndrome. Their partners were not overtly aware, but some of the women thought their partners had some awareness that they might be affected.

Group C consisted of ten NT women. These women's partners and children had not been diagnosed with Asperger syndrome, but the wives were completely convinced that their husbands did have it. The NT partners were quite well informed about Asperger syndrome, two of the women worked with children with AS and from the description and details they gave it appeared quite likely that their partners did have AS.

It cannot be categorically stated that the men in either groups B or C had Asperger syndrome, but it does need to be respected that the women are the ones who live with their partners twenty-four hours a day, and know them probably better than anyone else. They are the ones most likely to be aware that the problems occurring in the relationship may be due to their partner having Asperger syndrome.

The results of the study were quite disturbing. I have presented them in table 18.1.

Table 18.1 Awareness and Aspergers Syndrome			
	Group A %	*Group B* %	*Group C* %
No trust in partner with AS	0	40	70
Sexual problems	20	50	50
Physical health	20	66	80
Problems with children	40	66	90
Verbal abuse	10	66	30
Physical abuse	30	66	80

The first area I examined was whether the NT partner had any trust in the partner with AS. This might be trust in different forms, trust to be honest, trust to look after the children or just trust to take responsibility in the running of the house. The question did not include whether they could trust their partner to be faithful; this came under a different category.

Group A were couples that included a partner who had received a diagnosis for Asperger syndrome and accepted the condition. The NT partner said that in some way she trusted her partner. It may be that she trusted him in all areas, except for example in looking after the financial running of the house; it may be that she had total trust for her partner in every way. In Group B, however, forty per cent of the women said they did not trust their partners whatsoever and in Group C seventy per cent said they did not trust their partners. This is quite a large difference and as trust is considered a very important ingredient in a successful relationship it shows the difficulties that lack of acceptance of the syndrome must present. These are highlighted even more in the other areas I looked at.

Next I compared the couples' sexual problems between the three groups; these problems may be lack of sex, premature ejaculation, rigid routines or retarded ejaculation. I found that twenty per cent of Group A stated that they had problems sexually with their partner. This was less than half the number of those in Groups B or C, in which fifty per cent said they had problems. Sex is a form of communication and it is not surprising that this is affected when there is conflict in other areas of the relationship. Men with Asperger syndrome seem to be very affected in a sexual way when they are angry or feel criticized and sex is often the first thing on the agenda to cease when there is conflict or disagreement in the relationship.

I also asked each woman whether she felt her relationship with an AS partner affected her physical health. Only twenty per cent of Group A felt that their health had suffered as a consequence, which is low compared to the other two groups. In Group B sixty-six per cent said that they felt their health had suffered. Some of the illnesses mentioned were panic attacks, high blood pressure, insomnia, migraines and one woman even cited breast cancer. In Group C, eighty per cent of the women said they felt their partner having Asperger syndrome had affected their physical health. One of these women had suffered a complete mental and physical breakdown. Research by G. W. Brown in 1993 showed there were links between stress in relationships and mental and physical health. Those links are indicated quite strongly in my research, especially in the cases when the man denies he has Asperger syndrome and externalizes the blame for the problems on his partner.

I asked whether the women felt their partner having Asperger syndrome had caused any problems with the children. In Group A, forty per cent said that they felt the problems they had with the children were a direct result of Asperger syndrome. This seems high, but not in comparison to the sixty-six per cent of Group B. Both couples in Group A and Group B had children who had been diagnosed with Asperger syndrome so the difference between the groups cannot be put down to this. If this was the case, Group C should have very few problems at all because none of the children had been diagnosed. This was not the case, as ninety per cent of the women in Group C said that they were having problems with the children and that these were due to their partner having Asperger syndrome and not being aware of it or accepting it. This is a huge difference and very strongly suggests the importance of awareness and acceptance by the person in a relationship with AS.

The last two areas I looked at were verbal abuse and physical abuse, although both types of abuse come under the umbrella of domestic violence. Hester, Pearson and Harwin offered a definition for domestic violence in 1998. 'Domestic violence is any violent or abusive behaviour (whether physical, sexual, psychological, financial, verbal, etc) which is used by one person to control and dominate another with whom they have or have had an intimate relationship' (Hester, Pearson and Harwin, 1998). The first area of abuse I investigated was verbal, such as name-calling and language intended to put down or discredit the other person; the damage caused by verbal abuse is predominantly emotional. The second area was physical abuse. This may include shoves and restricting movement, pinching, slapping, punching, pulling hair, kicking and using objects to cause physical harm.

In Group A only ten per cent of this original sample said that their partners were verbally abusive towards them. This rose very sharply to sixty-six per cent in Group B, yet decreased to thirty per cent in Group C. This decrease in Group C is quite misleading as it could be interpreted as an improvement over Group B. This is not the case, as in Group C the verbal abuse seems to have been replaced by physical abuse. The cycle of violence often begins with more minor issues; an individual may begin by being verbally abusive towards his partner. Domestic violence is about power and control and is used to gain control over the other partner. If verbal abuse fails to achieve control then it can escalate into physical abuse.

Physical abuse was apparent in thirty per cent of couples in Group A; most of the cases cited were one-off incidents that the NT partner described as out of character and not involving severe violence. The rate of physical abuse doubled in Group B where there was a partner who denied he had Asperger syndrome and a child who had been diagnosed. This may because the partner with Asperger syndrome struggles with having a child whose behaviour probably reminds him of his own. The possibility that he may also have Asperger syndrome may have been questioned and the internal battle this caused may have increased his stress and anxiety levels.

Stress and anxiety levels are reported as being quite high in adults with Asperger syndrome, who are continuously struggling with a multitude of communication and social problems. Some AS adults can contain most of the anxiety it causes them but if the frustration reaches a level they can no longer contain and control then they can react violently. In most cases they will divert this anger onto some inanimate object, as was the case in most of the incidences reported in Group A. However, if an AS man is in denial it is often his partner who he blames for the problems they are having. This culminates in the anger and violence being directed at her and this can have very frightening and damaging consequences for the woman involved. Eighty per cent of the women in Group C had been subjected to physical violence, one case of which was long-term and chronic. Their partners showed little remorse for this and most had told her she deserved it.

There can be very little hope for these relationships if the man does not become aware and accept he has a problem and if he does not believe that his behaviour and actions towards his partner are completely unacceptable. A safe place for the NT partner to voice his or her feelings is FAAAS (Families of Adults afflicted with Asperger Syndrome) website, run by Karen Rodman for NT partners needing support and understanding. It offers 'a listening ear' to men and women who are struggling in AS relationships and in particular when their AS partners are in denial.

It is the relationships where the AS partner is in denial that are more likely to become abusive or violent. Chronic violence is extremely difficult to change within a relationship when the man does not have Asperger syndrome. In relationships where Asperger syndrome is present it could be even more difficult, especially if the man is in complete denial. His partner will probably be the only person who sees the abusive side of him; to the rest of the world he may appear kind, caring and thoughtful. He will be strongly trying to protect his own identity and will fight against the possibility that anything could be wrong with him. He will interpret almost everything his wife says to him as criticism and see her as the enemy to be fought against and controlled. For these relationships there is little hope of survival and unfortunately it is often hope that keeps the woman in the relationship, hope that he will change, hope that he will realize he has AS, hope that he will one day acknowledge all the pain and hurt she has suffered in order to try to make things work. Hope can be very strong and is often the last thing a woman in an abusive relationship gives up.

It is very unlikely that things will change in these dysfunctional relationships and the woman has a responsibility to herself and her children, if there are any. The effects of witnessing violence by children are of paramount significance and can cause long-term damage. Boys in violent relationships are more at risk of becoming violent themselves and girls are more likely to become victims. Staying for the sake of the children is a false and dangerous belief. The woman will need help and support in leaving the relationship and it is not uncommon for her to be stalked, intimidated and threatened by her partner. If the police and professionals are aware of the implications of Asperger syndrome they will be able to be more sympathetic and supportive to the woman.

If the couple are married and divorce becomes a reality, the problems this can present can also be very difficult to sort out. Lynn Henderson and Nicole Hackett, both solicitors, recently published an article that highlights some of the problems in a divorce case when one of the partners has Asperger syndrome. The paper, 'Aspergers syndrome in child contact cases', states that over the past few years the issue of Asperger syndrome is being raised more often. It highlights the importance of professionals being aware of this disorder and knowing how to deal with it if it arises. The authors discuss the similarity in the problems reported by the women they spoke to. Examples are given of bizarre and dangerous behaviour and the implications this can have on the divorce, custody of the children and the impact on the women. One recurring problem that women stated was their car being tampered with and made unsafe. I have also found examples of this in my own research and have highlighted the importance of awareness (Aston and Forrester, 2002).

These problems can occur during a divorce case whether or not the partner has received a diagnosis for Asperger syndrome. The biggest difference a diagnosis makes to a divorce case is that the woman will be believed when she describes some of her husband's bizarre and sometimes disturbing behaviour towards her. It is to be hoped that the professionals involved will increase their own awareness of the condition and then be able to deal with matters that arise in a more appropriate and constructive way.

Awareness of the partner with Asperger syndrome is an essential ingredient if the relationship is to survive on a level that is not abusive or fraught with problems. As awareness of Asperger syndrome increases so does awareness in the professional sector. The demand for adult diagnosis is growing and the need for psychologists and psychiatrists to specialize in this area is becoming evident. However, we still have a long way to go.

Key points

- If the couple is not aware of AS, it is likely that the NT partner will be blamed for most of the relationship problems.
- Some AS men will deny they have Asperger syndrome.
- If a man denies that he has AS, incidences of verbal abuse and domestic violence become more prevalent.
- Awareness of Asperger syndrome can allow understanding of the problems the couple have been experiencing.
- Individuals with AS can vary in the way the three core areas are affected.
- Initial research shows extreme differences in couples when the man is aware and has accepted he has AS.
- There is little hope for relationships when Asperger syndrome is denied or suppressed.
- Awareness of AS is essential if the relationship is to survive in a functional manner.
- It is often through the diagnosis of a child that parents first become aware that one of them may be affected by Asperger syndrome.

19

Diagnosis

Almost all the AS adults I spoke to felt that having a diagnosis and knowing that Asperger syndrome was the reason for the problems they had been experiencing came as a great relief. This was expressed quite strongly and not just as an advantage for them as individuals but also for their partners. Many of the men claimed that they now felt better understood by their partners and that their partners were able to make some allowances for the times when the men got it wrong.

The majority of the NT women felt far more able to cope once they understood what was causing the difficulties. They now knew what the problem was and no longer blamed themselves or felt that they were going mad. Now that she understood him better she was able to accept that he was not being selfish and uncaring.

Earlier in the book I talked about self-identity and Asperger syndrome. Many of the AS men I spoke to had developed a strong opinion of who they were and what they were like. Many said their partner had accused them of being selfish and they felt this was a total injustice. From their perspective, they were trying very hard to do what was best for their partners. They were unaware what it was they were getting so wrong and, before the discovery of Asperger syndrome, blame had often been placed on their partner.

It probably, therefore, comes as quite a relief to both partners to learn there is a cause for the difficulties. It externalizes responsibility away from the individual. One man said Asperger syndrome became the bogeyman, the demon; it became responsible for all the problems they had now and in the past. It often comes as a tremendous relief to have a reason and a hanger for blame.

Chris and Gisela Slater-Walker's book *An Asperger Marriage* covers the subject of diagnosis thoroughly. Chris, who has been diagnosed with Asperger syndrome, writes how he felt that the discovery of AS would have a positive effect on their relationship: 'It would give us a basis on which to make a properly guided attempt to live a meaningful life together.'

This way of feeling is shared by a majority of the AS men I have come into contact with. A man who had been diagnosed said that not only could his partner now understand that he had not meant to be cruel or unkind, but it also helped both of them understand why he had not realized the pain he had been causing her. He had not been aware that she had felt hurt. He also said that the diagnosis had a downside to it, and now felt that it had placed the whole weight of the relationship on his shoulders. He could no longer blame her, or the family or anything else; whatever went wrong it was his fault because he was the one with the deficit. This was quite a sad perception and it was obvious from reading his wife's response that she had no idea about the way he felt. It was a subject that he had not discussed with her because, he said, he felt he was under so much pressure that it was taking everything he had to keep things under control.

His wife expressed the extreme loneliness she felt because her distant and uncommunicative husband never shared any of his feelings with her. She blamed this totally on Asperger syndrome and said she thought it was simply because he did not feel. His account showed that this was actually far from the truth; he had plenty of feelings, very sad ones and a feeling of hopelessness that he did not share with her.

For other men, a diagnosis gave them the chance to work on improving some aspects about themselves they now realized were not quite right, for example, eye contact, not interrupting and thinking before they spoke. The lengths that many men and women with Asperger syndrome were prepared to go to in order to be more acceptable in society were surprising and some have worked very hard on improving their eye contact and remembering to look directly at someone when talking to them. They also needed to learn it was OK to look away every now and then, but to look interested when in dialogue with another and to also maintain eye contact.

On the other hand Chris Slater-Walker (*An Asperger Marriage*) admitted that since his diagnosis some of his AS traits seemed to have degenerated, and that this may be because he now has a reliable excuse not to have to participate in the social activities he did not care for.

Some felt it enabled them to find support; this may have been through the National Autistic Society or from a website such as ASPIRES, which offers a great source of help and support to those with Asperger syndrome and their partners.

One man said a diagnosis had opened many doors to him and he was now able to make choices as to what to do about it. It enabled him to work at using different strategies and ways of showing his feelings. His NT partner could understand that he showed his love for her in active ways, like making her breakfast in bed on a Sunday and doing the tasks she gave him. He wanted her to know he cared for her but had not been able to offer this in an emotional way.

Eighty-six per cent of the AS men and women felt their relationship had improved considerably since they had received a diagnosis and they felt more understood and accepted. The relief they had found was expressed quite strongly. Unfortunately, when reading the accounts from their NT partners, it appeared that some of them did not share the same feelings of being understood. Although the diagnosis allowed their AS partners to feel more or better understood, they did not themselves feel more understood by them. The main advantage for them was that their partner did not always interpret everything they said to him as criticism and were more able to accept that they might conceivably be making a valid point.

A woman whose husband has now received a diagnosis sent me the account below. It is very moving and explicit and gives an accurate description of the difference a diagnosis can make in some relationships. I have omitted any factual information that might be identifying, this is shown by [ ].

My husband and I commenced seeing a psychiatrist at the end of [ ] and he was diagnosed with Aspergers syndrome in [ ]. I was absolutely desperate at the time and said if we didn't get help I would not be able to take living in a marriage like ours anymore. From his point of view he didn't think there was anything wrong.

After the diagnosis I felt validated and affirmed. I have come out of a long dark tunnel. I have peace that I didn't have before and the sense of relief was enormous. It has given me great comfort. I wasn't losing my mind, there had been something wrong and it wasn't my fault. My feelings were real, true and justified. I was a normal woman who's emotional, mental and physical needs had not been met in a marriage that made me feel like I was living in a freezer. I found my husband to be cold, unemotional, indifferent, detached, seemingly stubborn, unresponsive and uncaring about my needs and feelings. The loneliness was unbearable. He was not even a companion. He seemed to have absolutely no idea what I was talking about when I tried to speak to him about emotional intimacy and bonding or the needs of our children or myself. He said he did not understand what I was talking about. He felt that my needs were in fact unreasonable and unrealistic expectations. I suffered cruel emotional abuse, intended or not is not the issue, the consequence, the reality of living with someone who has Aspergers syndrome stripped me of who I am. My husband did not want my emotions, my feelings, my body, my thoughts or my opinions, the very essence of who I am as a person. I felt unloved, unwanted, undesirable, in fact he had no need of everything that makes me a woman, a wife and a mother. The pain, anguish and despair were sometimes overwhelming. It was soul destroying. He was uninterested in me. I asked him why he married me and he kept saying it was because he loved me. Nothing made any sense.

I have found that since the diagnosis everything has fallen into place. All the years of pain, anguish and despair now made sense. My self-worth, self-esteem and confidence in myself has increased enormously. My soul is being restored. It has truly affirmed me as a human being and a woman. I feel that I have value and that my opinions are worthwhile. I have found that my identity is returning and I am not ashamed of my feelings and emotions anymore. The feeling of shame was enormous before the diagnosis. I felt reduced to less than a woman. I now feel free. Know the truth and the truth will set you free and that certainly applies to me. I have mourned and grieved over my dreams and expectations regarding marriage and the lack of emotional bonding with my husband but at least I now feel I have myself back. I felt stripped of who I was as a person and now I feel somewhat restored and I am growing stronger. I have decided to stay in this marriage, I am in for the long haul. I believe my husband now when he says that he loves me. Admittedly I still have to ask him but at least I know and understand now he does. I have put a lot of love, time, effort, pain, despair and anguish into the marriage and view it as an investment that has involved strength of mind and great courage. My husband respects me and he has positive traits and characteristics that I love and value. He can no longer deny there has been a problem. It is not a question of blame but rather one of survival. The survival of my sanity, a marriage that is now almost [ ] years old and my family of [ ] beautiful daughters, [ ] sons-in-law and [ ] lovely grandchildren.

My daughters have told me that they would not blame me if I had wanted a divorce. The diagnosis of Aspergers syndrome regarding my husband and their father has also helped them. They themselves now understand that their father does love them. He was just not able to show it or respond to them in the way they needed as they were growing up. They now know that they are worthy to be loved and they are more confident also. They respect him and are able to understand and love him. We now know what we are dealing with. It has strengthened our entire family.

As for the effect it has had on my husband. He experienced depression when he realized that in fact I was not unreasonable and he had Aspergers syndrome. He said he felt bad about the way he had treated me and he hoped he had not ruined my life. He seemed to go into denial soon after the diagnosis and did not want to talk about it. Maybe he had to step back to assimilate what had happened. He still finds it hard to talk about. I think he was also angry. It took some time for him to realize that people were not out to get him but in fact were trying to help. I hope he knows he is truly loved, wanted and respected. It is hard to talk to him sometimes. I have told him to embrace the good aspects of AS and we can work on the negative side of it together. I think he was relieved that certain areas of his life had an explanation. I admire my husband for the way in which he has coped with work although, as he finds it hard to communicate and does not pick up social cues easily, I don't know the reality of the situation. However I know he is respected for his knowledge and abilities. He is now also socializing at lunchtime with the people he works with. He has not told the people at his place of employment about the diagnosis, as there is a limited understanding of Aspergers syndrome in this country. The stigma attached to autism and the lack of awareness of the true nature of it in our society is daunting to say the least. I think we would be expecting too much from people to know how to deal with it appropriately in a way that would not affect the way they think about my husband or treat him. It would affect his credibility, undermine his authority and cause him unnecessary heartache. It would eventually affect his abilities and work in a detrimental way. I do not want to see him hurt, humiliated or patronized because of ignorance and a lack of understanding about Aspergers syndrome. He deserves to be honoured and treated with respect.

Our marriage has always had a very low priority for him, as has our relationship but now he has been confronted with the truth he is making more effort in that regard. I am very hopeful. I know now that he does love me and that makes it worthwhile. He seems to be more considerate and understanding towards me and I definitely feel a warmth he never used to show towards me. He still feels threatened when emotional demands are made on him but I think he understands what is happening more now.

This woman had found a direct benefit from her husband's diagnosis and this is often the case if the AS partner receives and accepts the diagnosis. It will still be a struggle for him to understand his partner's emotional needs, but at the very least she will be able to reconcile this by having a 'hanger' to blame it on – Asperger syndrome.

Three AS men in my study felt the diagnosis had come too late, and that their relationships had already fallen apart because neither partner had known or understood what was causing their problems. Both remorse and regret were expressed over this and the men felt very sad that their condition had not been recognized by one of the many professionals they had gone to for help, such as doctors, counsellors or psychotherapists. This emphasizes the importance of awareness and the need for professionals to understand the complexities of the syndrome. Many men and women I spoke to talk about the feeling of being different, alienated, rejected by society.

One man said that had he known he had Asperger syndrome, his partner and he could have been directed on to the right path and found ways to compensate for what was lacking in the relationship and caused their problems. The biggest problem was, he said, that they recognized it too late, and his wife had already left. This relationship had been under a lot of stress and this had certainly taken its toll on both partners. Stress in any relationship is likely to cause mental and physical problems and in my next chapter, I look at these effects of Asperger syndrome.

Key points

- The majority of NT women feel more able to cope after their partner's diagnosis.
- One AS man felt it meant that the relationship now depended on him and he could no longer blame others.
- Most AS men and women say a diagnosis helped them both to understand and to try to improve the relationship.
- One woman described the difference diagnosis has made for her relationship.
- A few AS men say that for them diagnosis came too late.

20

Mental and Physical Health and Asperger Syndrome

Two-thirds of the men in my study believed that their mental health had suffered as a consequence of being in a relationship and having Asperger syndrome. Forty per cent cited depression as the main mental health problem caused by the stress that the relationship created for them.

Tony Attwood, in his book *Asperger Syndrome: A Guide for Parents and Professionals*, describes how depression can appear in adolescence. He describes this as a time when the AS adolescent, although intellectually able, can often become the target for teasing when he tries to make friends. Other children soon sense that he is not socially able and might identify him as being odd or different, so he may find it hard to be accepted by his peers. The AS adolescent wants and needs to be liked and feel accepted, this rejection can cause him to feel shut out and depression can set in. It seems the harder he tries, the more he is rejected and the more depressed he will feel.

This is very similar to what happens when the adult with AS forms an intimate relationship with another and lives with his or her chosen partner. As in adolescence the AS adult is going through a time of transition and change, it is these times that can be most stressful for the AS individual. The same need to be liked and succeed is still apparent and many AS men have stated that they felt no matter how hard they tried to do the right thing they failed. Some talked about their failure to come up to their partner's expectations, others said they felt inadequate and pessimistic about the relationship. Most of the men had a genuine need to be liked and approved of, but this was hindered by the difficulties that Asperger syndrome presents in a relationship.

Many soon found that their efforts to win their partner's approval often failed and were met instead with sadness or anger and frustration. This produced stress and anxiety for many of the men, and the result frequently was depression. Two men stated that they believed that their depression was the direct result of how their partners reacted to them, especially if the reactions were anger or shouting. They felt criticized and victimized and as a result became depressed and reclusive. Although depression was cited fairly frequently by AS men, fifteen per cent of them still felt the relationship was worth it compared to the loneliness they had felt before. They discussed the longing they had felt to be accepted and needed. They felt that no matter how depressed they may feel now, it was far better than the way they felt when they were on their own and worried that they would never find a partner.

These intense and genuine feelings of needing to be wanted, liked and approved of probably relate to when the men were at school and the rejection and loneliness they had often felt at that time in their lives. One man talked about his life as a teenager at school. He had been very tall, and was the target for much name-calling; he had been severely bullied. Despite his height, he never retaliated and the school bullies soon realized they had nothing to fear from him. He was so afraid of his tormentors that he used to spend lunchtimes hiding in the toilets and eating his sandwiches in silence and fear. Sometimes the dinner ladies would discover him and being completely unaware of what was going on would send him outside to the playground where he received yet another verbal or physical beating. When he left school after his A levels he went to university to take a degree in accountancy. He had made up his mind before he arrived there that he was going to be different and tried to act out his life like the popular school clown who had made his life a misery in secondary school. He tried to act blasé and make jokes, most of which, unfortunately, offended people. Very quickly he found himself being avoided and ignored.

The crunch finally came when he became the target of a cruel joke by a girl he liked, when she agreed to meet him for a date. She went out with him to an expensive restaurant agreeing to pay half the bill. After the meal she sneaked out the back way leaving him to bear the cost. He was only a student and did not have enough money on him to cover it. The scene this caused at the restaurant was quite traumatic for him and his feelings of distress and trepidation increased when he discovered she was telling everyone he was gay. It all proved too much for him and, as a result, he became withdrawn and paranoid. Soon afterwards he suffered a complete breakdown, was admitted to a psychiatric hospital and had to leave university, giving up his degree.

He later formed a relatively good relationship with someone who cared for him very much. His new partner understood Asperger syndrome and both have tried very hard to make things work. He still unfortunately retained remnants from the past and sometimes misinterpreted what she was saying as a put down, retaliating by putting her down. This made her very unhappy and she told him how he made her feel. Consequently he became very depressed, describing himself as a hopeless failure who could not make his partner happy. He was prescribed anti-depressants, and recommended to me for counselling. When he felt ready, we were able to work on slowly making improvements to the relationship and the self-esteem of both partners.

Another area that can cause high stress levels is the need for strict and regimented routines, and the problems these can cause in the relationship was voiced by an AS man in his forties. He claimed that his stress was caused by his frustration in trying to get his partner to stick to the routines he required. He believed she actively went out of her way to disrupt his routines and make it difficult for him.

My research showed that although most of the men blamed themselves for their partners' unhappiness and felt they had failed their partners, they often, at the same time, blamed their partners for the way they felt depressed, and did not appear to see the two factors were connected.

Many of the NT women also claimed that they had suffered extreme stress, depression and two of the women said they had contemplated suicide. They claimed that this was a direct result of their relationship with their partner. They believed that their mental health had improved since they had discovered their partners had Asperger syndrome. This im-provement was increased by developing a greater and deeper understanding of what AS was and was not responsible for. One thing that did become apparent from the research was how little the men understood their partners' mental state and the reasons why they felt down or depressed. This lack of empathy meant that they did not know how to interpret or react to their partners' distress.

If the NT woman became emotional or depressed, it might be interpreted by her AS partner as a form of manipulation, trying to make him feel bad or responsible. The AS partner struggled with accepting that there does not have to be a logical reason for being upset and it was not always a form of manipulation. Some men reacted to their partners' tears with a total lack of response; they distanced themselves, simply not having any idea what to do. Others may respond with anger or contempt in an endeavour to stop their partners' crying.

When one woman cried in the counselling room because she had fallen out with her daughter and some harsh words had been voiced between them, her husband completely ignored her. I asked him why he just stared ahead and did not offer her any comfort or sympathy.

'She doesn't want it!' he said. 'If I try to go near her she will just reject me.'

I asked him why he thought she would do that.

He said, 'Because if she cries then it means I have done something wrong and it is safer not to say anything.'

I explained that she was crying over what had happened with their daughter and might need some support to help her feel better. He leaned towards her and quickly touched her hand and then withdrew, it was an action without any affective display. He was at a complete loss as to what to do and could only remember the times when she was upset over something he had done.

An adult with Asperger syndrome has tremendous problems interpreting what non-verbal signs mean, and understanding emotional expression and knowing how to react to it. He does not know what to say or do in an emotional situation so will often do nothing at all or try and do a practical chore like cleaning his partner's car or making her a cup of tea. He is trying to show he cares in a practical and more objective way. He finds this far easier than trying to figure out what he is supposed to do to emotionally support her.

Most of the women with Asperger syndrome talked about the frustration and anger that being in a relationship caused them, with one-third reporting that they thought it made them depressed. Depression is often anger turned inwards and many of the AS women I interviewed were able to express and display their anger a lot more easily than the AS men. This may account for the gender difference I found in depression in the AS adults – depression was ten per cent higher for AS men than for AS women. The AS men were far more likely to internalize the anger they felt towards their partners than the AS women. Not all the men in my research, though, felt the relationship had had a negative effect on them.

One-third of the men I contacted felt quite the opposite about their mental health and physical health and said that they felt both had greatly improved since they had been in a relationship. They gave various reasons for the improvement they felt. One man said that due to his partner's profession she had been able to teach him ways to eliminate stress, eat better and exercise. Another said his wife would massage his forehead when he was stressed and he would close his eyes, he said he found this helped him to relax. Some of them said they felt better simply because they were in a relationship and not alone anymore.

It did appear on the whole that most men needed and preferred to be in a relationship and this did not always depend on how happy the relationship was. The important factor seemed to be about being in the relationship. Some would completely dismiss the fact that both partners were desperately unhappy, as long as the relationship was maintained. I spoke to one couple struggling with a relationship that had completely broken down. He lived his life totally separate from her, he would not involve her in anything he did, spent hours and hours at work, kept her separate from his business life and did not ever take her out. She lived a very lonely life and he only had sex with her to have children, otherwise he never physically touched her. He did not talk to her and when at home just shut himself in his library.

The problems had become unbearable and the woman could not cope with the loneliness anymore. They had had two children; the second child had died from meningitis when he was six months old. Her eldest, a girl, had been diagnosed as being on the autistic spectrum. Her husband had decided to complete the family; they were to have another child and he hoped this would be a boy. She had refused to have sex with him and said she could not live with him under his conditions anymore. Her threats to divorce him had provoked him into seeking help from counselling.

It had been suggested to him when his daughter was diagnosed that he was also affected by Asperger syndrome, and although he accepted this, he would not allow his wife to discuss it, as he believed she would use it as a weapon to undermine him. He stated quite strongly that he did not believe talking to a stranger would help but if it convinced his wife that she should have another child and stay with him, then he was prepared to come along to counselling. He hoped this would help her sort her problems out and stop her constant criticism of him just because he wanted to keep the family together.

This man could not see the misery around him; all he could focus on was the family he was trying to create and the importance of maintaining it. He was also very unhappy and because he blamed his wife for his unhappiness he had tried solving it by keeping away from her and not allowing her into his life. He could not see that it was his distance that was making her so unhappy, his need for the family was all he focused on and was far more important to him than his happiness or hers.

When working with cases like this it is vital to try and change the direction of the AS man's focus, but this can be very difficult at times. If this is the case it is sometimes better for the woman to consider if the relationship is worth the unhappiness it is causing her, especially if he is not prepared to accept the problems that having AS causes in a relationship.

The AS men in my research were also asked whether they felt having Asperger syndrome and being in a relationship had caused them any physical problems. Fifteen per cent replied that they felt the stress it had caused had had a direct effect upon their sexual performance. Two also claimed it had caused them to gain weight and they no longer felt happy with themselves.

Sex is frequently the first thing to suffer in a relationship if there is stress and anger between the couple. Problems between the couple can cause the AS partner to feel under pressure and because of the frequent anger he is harbouring the stress affects his sex drive and performance.

The AS women in my research believed that having AS and being in a relationship had had a severe and detrimental effect on either their mental or physical health. All claimed at times to feel highly stressed and anxious as a result of the relationship. There were also claims of various health problems that they felt were a consequence of this. These ailments included weight loss, high blood pressure and palpitations.

The AS women seemed far more aware and concerned than the AS men about the problems and complications in the relationship. They would look for ways to solve these problems and be bitterly disappointed if they failed. All the AS women in my research also lived with men who were on the autistic spectrum. They carried a lot of the responsibility for the relationship in a very similar way to the NT women I contacted.

All the NT women in the relationships stated that their mental and sometimes physical health had suffered as a consequence of being in a relationship with an AS man. Many of the NT women were on or had been on anti-depressants; they reported feeling exhausted, frustrated, desperate and lonely and many thought they were going mad. For some, this changed once their partners had been diagnosed or they became aware of what was causing the problem. After the realization that the difficulties were due to Asperger syndrome, and they were not responsible for their partners' lack of emotional response and input into the relationship, they felt they could begin to build up their self-esteem. Once they understood that their AS partner simply *could* not provide any emotional support, rather than *would* not, matters began to improve. Awareness of the syndrome can have a positive effect on the couple's relationship and if help is sought and the couple's awareness and understanding of the syndrome is increased, many of the mental and physical problems may be alleviated for both partners.

Many couples who are unhappy or concerned about their relationship approach counselling agencies for help and support. Many couples affected by AS at some time travel down this road, either alone or together. The next chapter investigates the outcome of some of the journeys they have made.

Key points

- The majority of AS men believe that their mental health suffers as a consequence of being in a relationship and having Asperger syndrome.

- Many AS men say they have at some point suffered from depression.

- Many AS men feel their mental health has improved since being in a relationship.

- A number of AS men say that, despite the problems, they preferred being in a relationship to being alone.

- Stress can be caused by trying to maintain rigid routines as AS adults often do.

- Many NT partners claim they suffer extreme stress and depression.

- Many AS women said the relationship had made them feel depressed.

- Many AS men said their mental and physical health had improved since starting the relationship.

- A number of AS men claim that their sexual performance had been affected by the relationship and having AS.

- AS women say that their physical health suffers because of their relationship.

- Some couples feel their health has improved since diagnosis of AS.

21

Counselling and Asperger Syndrome

Seventy-five per cent of the couples I contacted had at some time been for couples counselling. Some had returned to counselling on many occasions and had spent vast sums of money trying to find the help they needed to discover the solution to their relationship problems. Unfortunately, for most of these couples, counselling had not worked and sixty per cent had been left feeling totally dissatisfied: for some the relationship was in a worse state than it was before.

The main reason for this is lack of awareness. Unless the counsellor and the couple had been aware that Asperger syndrome was present, and understood the mechanics of AS and the problems it caused within a relationship, the counselling habitually failed. For example if the counsellor is unaware that the man is affected by Asperger syndrome, then she will not have a clear and true perspective of the couple in front of her (for convenience I am presuming the counsellor is female).

For instance, the AS man may be on his best behaviour. He may appear very meek and polite, telling her in a quiet voice that he tries his best to make his wife happy, that he does all the jobs for her and gives her his wages and all she does is criticize him. The counsellor may interpret his lack of eye contact as low self-esteem or shyness, and she may be touched by his boyish and almost coy attitude. The NT woman on the other hand, may appear neurotic, complaining, frustrated, demanding and angry. She will be desperate to tell the counsellor how she feels and what the relationship is doing to her. The counsellor may soon find herself being drawn into the role of his rescuer.

One couple went to see a counsellor about their communication problems and the man's refusal to have any physical and sexual contact with his partner. They had been together for ten years and the relationship had deteriorated since he had lost his job. The woman was very frustrated and told the counsellor how difficult it was to live with him and how she received a bare minimum from the relationship. After listening, the counsellor then asked the husband for his perspective and he replied that he felt that he had contributed greatly towards the relationship and had obviously failed. He then added that his wife was unhappy because he could not afford to take them on holiday abroad. The woman was very angry at this statement and said she had already paid for their holiday away. The counsellor asked why the woman was feeling so angry.

'Why do you think I am so angry?' she almost screamed. 'He just can never see my point of view, I really think I am going to go completely mad!'

To this the counsellor said, 'If the situation is so untenable why have you stayed with him?'

The impact of this question was negative and damaging for both partners and they did not return to counselling. The woman felt she was not believed and that the counsellor had sided with her husband. I have heard of many counter-productive comments by counsellors who simply did not understand the issues pertaining to a couple where Aspergers syndrome was part of the equation and were totally misled by the ambiguous signs that the syndrome can give.

One woman recalled how a counsellor had asked her if she was gay, as she seemed to have such a problem dealing with normal male behaviour. Counselling can be very damaging to the relationship if Asperger syndrome is interpreted as 'normal' male behaviour. The difference between Asperger syndrome and the behaviour of NT men is that NT men have a choice in the way they behave; they can choose to talk to their partners or support them emotionally. Men with Asperger syndrome do not have this choice; they do not have the ability to know what is required of them. If the counsellor does not acknowledge this difference in the woman's partner, the woman is potentially left feeling unheard and not believed. It will feel as though the counsellor has just reinforced the AS man's behaviour towards his partner and now the NT partner will never be able to get him to see the part he plays in the relationship problems.

If the counsellor puts demands on the AS man to communicate more and talk about his feelings he may feel pressured into entering into dialogue that he finds extremely difficult. One man was told he had to spend five minutes every day talking about his emotions to his wife. He could not do this because he had no idea of what he was supposed to talk about and certainly no concept of what emotional conversation meant. He could not complete the task and the counsellor asked him why he could not talk about his emotions.

'I don't know,' he answered honestly.

'Well, maybe you can give it some thought and we will talk about it next week' the counsellor told him.

He felt very anxious and pressured by this; his wife kept prompting him to think about what he was going to say. When it came to the next session he did not show up and his wife had to go alone. He had switched off his mobile and she could not contact him. He did not go back to counselling, which was sad because he had, initially, been willing to try. Only when it was discovered he had Asperger syndrome did they go back to counselling together. They saw a counsellor who understood Asperger syndrome and was able to give them both more appropriate tasks to practise.

One woman with AS felt very let down by the counselling and psychotherapy services she had come into contact with. She had spent three years in psychotherapy with a psychotherapist who did not recognise she had Asperger syndrome. In this time she was subjected to some very deep and emotive work. She was pressured into analysing herself and her emotions. She would get very angry with the psychotherapist and was questioned over this anger. The psychotherapist decided the anger must be because the woman had been suppressing her deep fear of being rejected. This, the client was told, was linked to her childhood and how her father had been very distant. Her distant father had not bothered her in the past but now she had to think about it. She was having problems with her own children at the time and she felt the psychotherapist was suggesting she was a bad mother because of her difficulty in being affectionate with her children. The stress and anxiety she felt increased and self-perpetuated; she blamed herself for everything that was going on around her. She soon sank into a very deep depression caused by her attempts to suppress the anger she felt. One night she hit rock bottom, tried to commit suicide and was admitted to a psychiatric hospital after having a nervous breakdown. She was fortunate that, whilst she was in hospital, it was recognized by her psychologist that she had Asperger syndrome. The net result is that now she and her family are working together through the problems that are present within the relationship in a more constructive manner with an understanding of the syndrome.

I cannot emphasize enough the damage that may be caused in counselling if there is no awareness of the syndrome. It is of paramount importance if counselling is going to benefit the couple. Most of the couples I contacted who had been to counselling in the past reported it as a very negative and unproductive experience. In almost all these cases neither the counsellor (or psychotherapist) nor the couple knew that Asperger syndrome was present.

The feedback I received about counselling was not entirely negative but the thirty-one per cent of positive reports came from the AS men, not their partners. One man was pleased that counselling seemed to offer him a safe place to talk and enjoyed the neutrality that counselling offered. Another said that counselling assisted in explaining some of his solitary behaviour to his wife. The counsellor had decided that his problems were due to him being an only child. Although this was not the fundamental cause of his difficulties and the fact that he had Asperger syndrome was not recognised during the counselling, it did offer them an explanation for the lack of intimacy in the relationship. This had helped, he said, but did not offer them any long-term solutions. Once the counselling finished, the problems remained the same; nothing had changed, except that he understood more about the impact that being an only child can have.

Some NT women felt relieved to be able to voice their concerns to someone else and just being empathized with came as a relief for them. Some of the AS men said they enjoyed the attention and time the counsellor gave them. They felt the counsellor had controlled the equality of participation by the couple and one young man had said that it allowed him to talk without his wife finishing his conversations for him. On a different note though, one man felt the counsellor was as hostile towards him as his wife was. He felt he was victimized because he was male and the counsellor sided with his wife and did not want to hear what he had to say.

In addition to couple counselling, many of the couples tried individual counselling. Once again, if the counsellor is unaware of Asperger syndrome, counselling may be unsuccessful and only offer transient relief. This is particularly important when it is the AS man who is having counselling alone, especially if he is going to try and sort out the problems in his relationship. Because he is only able to offer his perspective of his relationship, the counsellor could end up with a very biased view, far removed from the truth. He will not be able to tell the counsellor that he cannot offer his partner any emotional support, and that he does not participate in anything she wants them to do together. He will not tell her, because he will not see this as the root cause of the problems he is experiencing. He will not be trying to fool the counselor: he cannot explain to the counsellor an issue that he is not aware of. If the counsellor is unaware that he has Asperger syndrome she will not get an accurate and honest picture of his problems and will not know the right questions to ask him. Her words of sympathetic encouragement will simply reinforce his belief that it is his partner who is wrong and he will do nothing at all to change his behaviour at home or try to understand his partner.

Some types of counselling involve looking into the past and encourage the client to revisit past feelings of anger. They encourage releasing control. Control over feelings is very important to individuals with Asperger syndrome and needs to be encouraged rather than challenged. It is this control that prevents some of the anger outbursts that can occur. Therefore therapies that dig up the emotions and actively encourage a person to relive old repressed feelings of anger, pain and hurt can be damaging to a person with Asperger syndrome, though they may be highly effective and productive in cases with NT individuals. To evoke such strong feelings and encourage the AS person to feel anger can be potentially dangerous and damaging.

One woman described how she had been to counselling with her fiancé. At the time both the couple and the counsellor were completely unaware that her fiancé had Asperger syndrome. The counsellor asked him about his childhood and suggested that maybe that was where his problems were rooted.

He objected very strongly to this, got up and stood in front of the counsellor saying how dare she suggest that there was anything wrong with his childhood. He picked up his coat and left the room. The counsellor was clearly shaken by his reaction; she had triggered a feeling in this man that he could not cope with. It was never discovered what had caused it, but it is likely that he misinterpreted what she was suggesting and perceived it as trying to apportion the blame on his childhood. If his childhood was not a pleasant time for him, he would react to her question in the way he probably reacted back then, by having a tantrum and walking out of the room, slamming the door behind him.

Another aspect of counselling raised by one man I spoke to was understanding what the counsellor was saying or asking. The person with AS will rarely comprehend innuendoes, double meanings and subtle suggestions. Difficulty in understanding what is being suggested by the counsellor is extremely difficult for the AS person. Unless the counsellor can talk to him in a very direct and clear way, he will struggle with understanding any hidden meaning. This problem is exacerbated in counselling as much of the communication is often about feelings.

A large proportion of the couples I spoke to mentioned feeling misunderstood and let down by the counsellor's lack of knowledge. Counselling couples and individuals affected by Asperger syndrome demands a very different type of technique than is offered to counsellors in typical training. If the counsellor has no awareness of Asperger syndrome, then the counselling is potentially damaging to both partners. Only reading a book about Asperger syndrome is not sufficient. AS is a serious condition. It is not a mental illness that can be cured or helped by taking medication; it is a brain abnormality, it is a developmental disorder, it is thinking in a different way. It is imperative that the counsellor understands this difference.

Asperger syndrome is a complicated condition that at times is not given the respect it deserves. This may be because it does not affect the individual's academic intelligence, it does not make the individual look any different or necessarily prevent them from working. Asperger syndrome is invisible and often only the people closest to the individual will be aware how disabling it can be. Lack of support for families faced with a diagnosis of Asperger syndrome is nationwide, possibly worldwide, and all professional agencies need to review their polices and incorporate support and services to families and individuals affected by this socially debilitating syndrome.

Counselling services and independent counsellors owe their clients the highest level of service possible. Hopefully in the future these services will be available to all adults with Asperger syndrome and their partners and family.

Key points

- The majority of AS couples have been for couples counselling.
- The majority of these feel dissatisfied with the counselling.
- NT women are sometimes left feeling not believed or feeling that the counsellor took sides with their partners.
- If the counsellor is unaware that AS is the problem, counselling may put extreme pressure on the AS partner.
- Many of the positive reports about counselling come from men with AS.
- Some types of therapy can be quite damaging to the person with AS.
- The awareness of AS among counsellors and counselling agencies needs to be increased.

22

Women and Asperger Syndrome

Up to now I have referred mainly to the male adult with AS. This is because the majority of my sample was male and, as Asperger syndrome appears to affect men predominantly, it made this book more straightforward and easier to comprehend if the AS adult was presumed to be male.

However, this highlights that a lot less is known about AS women than AS men. Within my research, however, I did receive replies to my question-naires from a small sample of women and that, coupled with the interviews and encounters with AS women I have had, forms the basis of this chapter. It needs to be mentioned though that this sample was relatively small and should not be used as a generalization of the wider population of AS women.

National studies in Great Britain claim that men commit ninety to ninety-seven per cent of reported domestic violence, which implies that women commit only three to ten per cent of reported cases of domestic violence. These figures may be misleading, as they are only based on reported cases and it seems less likely that a man will report a case of violence against him, partly due to the social stigma from being perceived as weak.

My research into relationships affected by Asperger syndrome showed that in seventy-five per cent of cases, the woman with Asperger syndrome was physically abusive towards her partner. This is a large percentage compared to the recorded national average and it does indicate (but not confirm) that AS women are more likely to be physically abusive towards their partner than NT women.

My research also highlighted different traits of AS men and AS women. One of the differences I found appears to be linked with identity. 'Who am I?' or 'What is the real me?' are questions asked far more by women with AS than men with AS.

Dr Tony Attwood (1998) noticed that girls with Asperger syndrome appeared to be able to 'follow social actions by delayed imitation'. In other words, AS girls are able to observe and imitate social actions, but often the timing of these actions is not so accurate or natural. AS women can often pick up a part or a role from watching TV, or by observing someone else. The person they imitate is often perceived as being popular and they will adopt their mannerisms, quotes and idiosyncrasies. AS women need to be liked and accepted, just like AS men, but the drive to achieve this seems much stronger.

AS men appear to establish at an early stage who they are and then stick to this quite rigidly. AS women, on the other hand, try out and experiment with different personas. Their drive and stamina in this are quite amazing, but it can also be quite exhausting for them. This appears in some cases to increase the likelihood of mood swings that can fluctuate from an incredible high to a very deep low.

Different women seem to conduct their search in a variety of ways. For some it may be religion, for others education and for some it may be different relationships. One woman I spoke to had turned to religion in order to try and find herself. She had travelled across the world doing this, she had lived in Tibet as a Buddhist, and she had spent time in America living as a Mormon. She had even lived a Muslim life in Turkey with a family she befriended. Now bearing in mind that this woman had been diagnosed with Asperger syndrome and had great difficulty interacting with people, to achieve so much was not an easy task for her. Her quest for self-discovery was so great that she had battled against her natural desire to be alone and travelled and mixed with many different people and cultures to try to find, as she described it, what made her feel 'whole'. Another woman dated men from different cultures; she used the Internet to meet men and believed if she could find the right culture and nationality for her, she would find inner peace.

This need to feel whole or find inner peace and acceptance of oneself seems to be a driving force in some women with Asperger syndrome. When they think they have found the key they are excited and elevated, wanting those around them to share and be a part of their new discovery. Their energy is amazing and their determination and focus is rock solid.

One woman discovered that she was a Capricorn and an article on birth signs had said that Capricorns were determined and hard working and, although they appeared cold and distant, really very loving and affectionate. She was absolutely elated as she told me that she had found the answer and now knew why some people thought she was different. She was overjoyed with her discovery. Before very long this lady was an expert on astrology, she knew all about the planets and could map and memorize anyone's birth chart. Everyone she encountered was met with the question, what was his or her birth date? Her knowledge on the subject was outstanding. This all came to an abrupt end when she met a man who broke all the rules and did not in any way conform to his birth sign and the knowledge she had acquired. He challenged her with a lot of scientific evidence that astrology was not always reliable. She was very disillusioned and became quite depressed and despondent for a while, until she read about yoga and how meditation could change her life. Then the whole cycle began again.

One of the reasons why women may search so hard in comparison to men is possibly because they are naturally more emotional. Women are said to be more inquisitive and enquiring about their feelings and this may be why most of the books written by people with Asperger syndrome are by women.

If one looks at the counselling profession and at psychology students one will find that there are far more women than men involved. Women do appear to be more self-seeking and this does not change with having Asperger syndrome, in fact I would go as far to say that AS exaggerates this need in women.

Most people with Asperger syndrome are aware that in some way they are different and when they discover they have AS it can answer many questions for them. Some will want to learn more about it and will go as far as to give public talks and lectures. Some feel that discovering they have Asperger syndrome answers all the questions they have wanted to ask.

Many AS women, though, still have a need or drive to attain complete self-discovery. These women want to feel whole and complete and some will dedicate their lives to trying to achieve that feeling. Sadly this may not be achieved as the answer to feeling complete and whole is within oneself; it is not out there waiting to be discovered. Asperger syndrome may leave the woman feeling she is not cohesive, perhaps not quite getting things right and is not truly accepted by those around her. This will drive her forward to keep searching and for many AS women the search can be life-long.

Constant searching can be very exhausting and the frustration it causes may be responsible for outbursts of anger and frustration. These can be displayed in verbal abuse or physical abuse, both of which are normally directed at the person closest to them. This can be the case for AS men as well as women, and I have encountered men who also fluctuate between high and low points and try to behave in different ways, but my findings showed it was more evident and frequent in women.

AS women seem to have far more frequent outbursts of both verbal and physical anger than the AS men I spoke to and this is likely due to a higher stress level. This stress is probably caused by society's pressure on them to perform in a certain way in order to feel accepted by others. This requires a lot of control and concentration, and the role can only be maintained for so long. It is likely that as soon as the woman feels safe within her own environment again, the control is lost and the anger may be directed at her loved one.

I also found that most of the women I spoke to with Asperger syndrome were in relationships with men who also had Asperger syndrome. This was very different from the men with Asperger syndrome, the majority of whom had formed a relationship with an NT woman.

Another observation I made was that the women with Asperger syndrome complained about their partners not understanding them in exactly the same way as the NT women complained. This suggests that AS women have higher emotional needs then AS men. They need to feel understood and appreciated just like NT women do. Having Asperger syndrome does not mean that they do not need to feel emotionally fulfilled and acknowledged. When they do not receive this emotional support they may feel out of control and frustrated with the lack of response.

AS women may try to exercise control over their partners. This is not because they are trying to gain power over them, but because they need to keep control over their own life and everything in it and their partners are not meeting their needs. AS men also try to keep control over their lives and their partners but many have a huge fear of confrontation and will do anything to avoid it. This can give the AS woman the upper hand as she is more likely to become angry at a quicker rate, which can send him running or into submission. Sometimes the AS man will do anything to keep the peace; this does not necessarily mean, though, that the AS woman is the one who gains all the control.

To give an example, I interviewed a couple where both partners had Asperger syndrome. He wanted her to go with him to a music evening that was being held at their local theatre. She did not want to go, but he would not leave the issue alone and was still trying to pressure her into going that evening. She retaliated and became very loud and abusive to him, and at this juncture he instantly backed down and took flight. He went straight to the theatre where he spent the evening listening to his music alone. He was very angry that she was not there but did not bring it up at all when he got home, for fear that she would shout at him again. His fear of her anger was very real and this gave her control over the situation. He would, though, often find ways of venting his anger towards her in a way that allowed him to silently take back some of the control her loud and audible anger took away from him. He would refuse to enter into dialogue with her on a subject that was important to her, for instance, an issue regarding the children. He would not give her an opinion, or would just say he did not know what should be done, his classic favourite being 'It's up to you what you do!' This left her feeling unheard, irrelevant and very much alone. He had gained back the control.

Women with AS can sometimes give the impression of being very happy; they can appear very jovial and childlike. They are often very expressive with their voices and seem to have heaps of get up and go. This is quite different from the sometimes sombre and more serious attitude shown by some AS men.

The majority of AS women expressed concern about their appearance or figure but they do not do it for the same reasons that an NT woman might express concern. Sometimes NT women will dress in a certain way to please their partners. AS women will dress mainly to please themselves, and in a manner that allows them to feel comfortable. They may dress and look in a way that makes them feel good, or helps them to fit into the particular role they are trying to depict. Most AS women do not appear to spend time worrying about their partners' thoughts regarding the way they look. They are, however, concerned with whether they are appreciated for the effort they make to try to look after their partners and families. They want their partners to know that it is difficult for them to fulfil their expected role and to appreciate what they do. Unfortunately, most of the men they are with also have Asperger syndrome and are often not aware of their partners' needs. This can cause a lot of stress for the AS woman in the relationship.

Some of the differences between AS men and women may be due to gender roles. It is commonly known that little girls like to please and will actively do things to please others, enjoying the praise and response it evokes. For boys, praise still plays a relevant role but the drive to please others is not so strong. Neither is the same expectation to please placed on boys as it is on girls. These expectations can be carried over into adulthood and women can once again be seen trying to please their partners and families by being 'good wives and good mothers'. They may have to perform practical tasks like cooking, cleaning the house, ironing and washing clothes. In addition to this, there are emotional demands made upon them, they are expected to know why Sally was quiet or whether Tommy is unwell. The pressure on women in society to care, nurture and please is far more profound than it is on men. Men are sometimes allowed to be distant and silent, they are not expected to remember everyone's birthday or whether someone needs a hug. These caring roles are often put on to the woman. For women who do not have Asperger syndrome, this can be a pressure, but for AS women the result can be a confusing nightmare. AS women do not have the automatic insight to know how to fulfil emotional needs and provide the natural insight and intuition that is required by the family around them.

The pressure that society and the family put on AS women can be profound and the depression and anxiety that result can also be profound. There is a high probability that this is the reason that verbal abuse and anger is often so much higher in AS women than in AS men.

Asperger syndrome alone does not make a person violent, abusive or aggressive. If it did then everyone with AS would come under this category, and the majority do not. What AS appears to do is exaggerate some of the worst as well as the best traits a person has. In other words, if a person has the potential to be a high achiever, having AS can exaggerate this trait. If the person has a low tolerance threshold then AS may increase the likelihood that this threshold will be reached and exaggerate the reaction to it. This 'exaggeration factor' appears to be both a disadvantage and an advantage of having Asperger syndrome.

Key points

- Many AS women search in many different ways to try to discover their true identity.
- Constant searching for answers can result in frustration and be responsible for anger outbursts.
- Women with AS complain that their partners did not understand them.
- AS women try to enforce tremendous self-control.
- AS women often appear to have plenty of energy and can be quite expressive.
- Some of the differences between AS men and women may simply be due to differences in gender and upbringing.
- The pressure society and the family places on AS women can be profound.

23

Disadvantages of Asperger Syndrome

As part of my research I asked adults with Asperger syndrome the following question:

> Do you feel that having Asperger syndrome has caused any disadvantages to the relationship? If yes, please be specific.

This question was different to the others on the questionnaire, as it included the words 'Asperger syndrome'. The answers I received were expressed in a different way than the answers to other questions in my research.

Up to this point, a lot of the replies I had received from the respondents had been defensive and some had been quite critical either of themselves or their partners. The majority externalized much of the blame for the difficulties in the relationship onto their partners.

The answers that were given to this question were quite profound and displayed insight and awareness into what the AS adults felt they could and not do as a consequence of having Asperger syndrome. They were very objective and did not blame their partners, themselves or their relationships. The focus was totally on Asperger syndrome. One of the differences I found was in the choice of words used. Answers to many of the other questions had contained a lot of *but* words, such as 'she says I am aggressive *but*', 'she says I am needed *but*'.

The *but* word appeared far less in the answers to this question. The responses were far more decisive and less ambiguous. In many cases, the replies held a strong element of sadness, such as the AS adults feeling that they were in a 'no hope' situation in so far as, whatever they did, there were certain things they would never be able to do or achieve.

One particular man said that having AS meant he could not be as affectionate as he wanted to be and that he did not know how to respond to his wife or guess what she wanted. Up until this point, he had shown a lot of anger towards his wife and had argued that she criticized him, constantly trying to make him feel inadequate. In reply to whether he felt he was disadvantaged, he gave a very clear answer, owning the problems in the relationship completely, and there were no *buts*! He used an analogy to paint a picture of his feelings – 'It is like trying to describe colours you have never seen because you are colour-blind.'

It would be very difficult to describe colour if your world had always been monochrome and, from the answers to my questions, this is exactly what it appears to be like for those with Asperger syndrome. They are expected to be able to translate the feelings and emotions of others, when they really do not know what they are translating because they do not have the empathy or ability to interpret them.

I remember a few years ago talking to a clinical psychologist who was working with adults with Asperger syndrome. He was quite convinced that he could teach his patients how to feel and empathize and this was his main focus in his treatment with them. He told me how he had been working with a young man who was quite severely affected by Asperger syndrome and seriously felt that this young man was learning to show emotions and understand the emotions of others. I questioned this and suggested that maybe the patient had learned what was required of him and was play-acting the role to achieve what the clinical psychologist wanted. The reply was in the negative – 'No', he said, 'he really is developing the ability to empathize.' I did not question this psychologist any more as I realized that it would be pointless, as he wanted to believe that his patient was getting better.

My argument is that if someone can get better and recover from Asperger syndrome, then they never had it in the first place. Asperger syndrome is a life-long disorder. The individual can learn strategies, ways of adapting and coping with the situations that living and working with other people present him, but he cannot learn to do something he does not possess the capacity for. No amount of therapy can give him the ability to use insight and naturally empathize with people close to him. The man who likened himself to someone who was colour-blind was quite accurate in his description and he showed a great awareness of himself and the disabilities that having Asperger syndrome presents.

Another man discussed how it affected his social skills and this in turn took away his confidence. Social skills are required every time we come into contact with another human being. We have to use them continuously, people judge others by how competent they are in these skills and the level of proficiency can make a huge difference, not just in personal relationships but also in interviews, getting work and in the wider arena.

It is an aspect of human behaviour to constantly evaluate and form opinions about others. Often the first impression is the most important and we are quick to categorize others by how adept and confident they seem. Without any conscious thought we observe eye contact, when a person smiles, how they talk, is it an interesting likeable voice or is it monotonous and boring? Many of us have at some time had to sit through a lecture or conference presented by someone who talked in a monotone voice and paused for too long. Paying attention to such lectures can be very hard. If the same lecture were presented by someone who repeated exactly the same words but in a captivating and vocally expressive voice the effect on the people in the audience would be very different and their attention span would last far longer.

It is very difficult for the person with Asperger syndrome to change the tone of his voice or the facial expressions he shows. Many people are concerned about their appearance and spend a great deal of time, effort and money in trying to look attractive. They go on diets, work on their bodies and spend money and time buying clothes. For some people this is their way of increasing their self-esteem and feeling valued, respected and liked by others. The AS adult cannot simply go on a diet or spend time at the gym to achieve this because, in many cases, it is his social skills that are lacking. These skills can be slowly improved upon with much effort, but he will forever be working at them and even then they will never be as good as they would have been if he was an NT adult.

I remember a friend being told she was dyslexic, and how horrified she was at the time. In her first question to the educational psychologist, she asked if this meant that she would never be as good at reading, writing and spelling as she could have been without dyslexia. The answer was yes; no matter what she did she would never be able to reach the level that she could have done if she had not been dyslexic. So although the diagnosis gave her a reason for why she had grown up thinking she was stupid and why she had problems verbalizing complicated words, it also took away the hope that she could get better.

This is the message that was coming across in the answers I received to my question. There was the acknowledgement and acceptance of having Asperger syndrome, and the sadness that some things would never get better.

One man said he felt that without Asperger syndrome he could have been a better person and stopped worrying all of the time about the things he could not do. He talked about how sad it made him that he could not get things right for his wife. Both this man and his wife were still hopeful but also accepted that some things would not change. His partner also spoke about what their relationship could have been like if he did not have Asperger syndrome. They shared a lot of hope that they would be able to sort things out and achieve a more 'normal' relationship. Basically what they were wishing for was what the majority of NT people take so much for granted.

Some of the replies expressed that they felt having Asperger syndrome gave them a need to have time alone and be separate from the rest of the family. One man said that this separation could be simply reading alone or going away on business trips. Finding a balance between autonomy and intimacy can be a problematic issue in any relationship, but can often be a major problem in relationships affected by Asperger syndrome. It is a difficult balance to achieve and is dependent on a number of factors, a major one being how secure each person feels.

When some people talk about their relationship they describe how it makes them feel whole and complete. They may say they have found their other half and now feel whole. This is not viewed as a beneficial way of thinking in relationships and is an issue that often raises its head in counselling. If someone is the other half of a person and they make him or her feel whole, what is going to happen when they disagree or one partner is not there? The other person will then feel incomplete, no longer whole.

These feelings may be common in the early stages of a relationship or what is known as the passionate stage, which lasts for about the first six months. After this though, the relationship should develop into a deeper, caring stage and being apart should be easier and less painful. If not, the stress it can cause will have a negative effect on the relationship.

A functional healthy relationship is two whole people coming together and making two wholes, they should be like the two pillars that stand on a solid foundation at the right distance apart, so they can equally support the relationship above them. However, if one partner is insecure, then being apart and allowing distance will be especially difficult. It is more likely to be the NT partner who has feelings of insecurity brought on by some of the aspects of living with an AS partner.

Having Asperger syndrome can make it difficult for a person to express his feelings either verbally or non-verbally. This can leave the NT partner feeling unsure as to how much she actually means to her partner and as to what he is thinking about her. There is a selection of AS men for whom to say 'I love you', is a rare utterance. It is also rare to hear them offer any other statements of affection that will reveal the extent of their feelings towards another. The lack of eye contact and inappropriate facial expressions can give the impression of evasiveness. The lack of information the AS man gives about his working day can lead the NT partner to suspect that there may be something he is not telling her or hiding from her. This can lead her to feel insecure and unsure as to what he is doing or thinking. If this happens and the problem is not resolved, she may feel reluctant to give him much freedom. The more she tries to prevent his natural need for space and autonomy, the more he will withdraw; the more he withdraws the less freedom she will give him. The couple will now become locked in a vicious and destructive cycle.

The NT woman may find it difficult to understand why her partner would want to spend so much time alone. Often it is only when the woman develops a full understanding of Asperger syndrome that she is able to appreciate that this is a consequence of the condition and not because he is being dishonest, hiding something or not wanting to be with her. All individuals are different and have different needs, for some AS men this need for space will be stronger than in others.

Many NT women say that if only they could have quality time with their partners when they were together, then they would be able to tolerate the times when they were apart or their partners were distant. The problem of not being able to offer their partners quality time was also voiced by most of the men, who described it as one of the disadvantages having Asperger syndrome caused them.

One man wrote that he believed Asperger syndrome was responsible for the problems he and his wife had in communication. He said it prevented him from making the simple chitchat that he had observed in other couples. He said they had to repeat things to make sure they understood each other; this made trying to communicate very tiring for both of them. He said he wished he were able to make simple talk while they ate dinner. This man was very aware that the problems they were having were a direct result of Asperger syndrome, he did not blame his wife or himself.

This account highlights some of the tremendous difficulties that can be caused by having Asperger syndrome and reinforces the difference that awareness and acceptance of this condition can make in a relationship.

Communication difficulties was raised as a prime problem caused by Asperger syndrome in the relationship. Almost all the AS partners stated how much they wished that they could communicate more efficiently and be understood.

Another man believed that Asperger syndrome had caused him to lose his children and he felt dismayed that he had not been understood. His marriage had broken up as a result of communication problems and his inability to express to his wife how he felt and fulfil her emotional needs. He said he had tried very hard to keep things together, but neither he nor his wife had been aware at the time that he had Asperger syndrome. Eventually, she moved out with the children. His teenage children were angry with their dad and felt he could have done more to hold things together. He sensed their anger and avoided seeing them, because he believed they did not want to see him. By the time his wife discovered that he had Asperger syndrome and he received a diagnosis, it was too late. There was too much damage to rebuild the relationship. Since the diagnosis there has been a better understanding between him and his ex-wife but his children have never contacted him and have excluded him from their lives. His sadness over this is quite apparent and he blames this on Asperger syndrome.

The final disadvantage reported was that there was no one to actively assist in dealing with AS after patients received a diagnosis. One man had been diagnosed with AS quite late in life and was struggling with what it meant for him. At the time of diagnosis, all he had been given was a single page on the subject. He had read the information given to him, which basically told him that he had problems in particular areas. He recognized this was probably why his wife never seemed happy with anything he did, but there was nothing on the sheet as to what he could do about it. He felt confused, bewildered and lost. This was all the information he was offered – no advice or support to help him with these problems. All he had was an A4 sheet of paper to read and a diagnosis.

I also spoke to his wife, who herself was elderly. She had been trying to find out more information, and she also said that she felt very let down by the professionals and felt she and her husband should have been offered more advice and some support to help them both come to terms and deal with the diagnosis. She argued that if he had been told he had manic depression or schizophrenia then he would have been offered a follow-up session or counselling at the clinic. She argued that due to the fact he was not obviously disadvantaged by having Asperger syndrome, it was presumed that he, his wife and their family could cope without counselling.

Key points

- The answers to the question 'Do you feel that having AS has caused any disadvantages to the relationship?' were quite profound and offered much insight into Asperger syndrome.

- Awareness of the difficulties Asperger syndrome caused is clearly expressed by AS adults.

- Many expressed sadness in the knowledge that there were some things the AS adult could not do or improve.

- ○ Finding a balance between autonomy and intimacy can be a major problem in AS relationships.
- ○ Dismay was expressed at the lack of support offered to those with AS.

24

Benefits of Asperger Syndrome

The second question I asked directly about Asperger syndrome was whether the individual felt it had brought him or her any benefits.

Sixty per cent answered in the negative to this question. The other forty per cent found at least one advantage from having Asperger syndrome. I could find no obvious differences between those who found a benefit and those who did not. So what are the benefits of having Asperger syndrome according to the people who have it?

One man said it helped him to concentrate and focus, he said he had achieved a lot through hard work, determination and a single focus, which he related directly to having Asperger syndrome. At work his ability to focus enhanced his work performance. His staying power and absolute competence in the tasks he undertook were admirable. This is not uncommon in AS if the individual is lucky enough to find work in a field that they enjoy and are interested in. This man, though, took a notoriously long time to complete some of his tasks, but the end result was perfection.

There is often an edge of perfectionism in any job undertaken by someone with Asperger syndrome. He may take great pride in doing things the correct and most efficient way. This unfortunately does not always go down well with his co-workers, who see it as crawling up to the boss or, very often, as making the work they produce look inferior. The AS man, however, will not be able to do things any differently and if he is expected to cut corners to save time or keep in with his co-workers he will feel very pressured. It is unlikely he will be able to complete a job in a way that he finds inferior; he will only change to a way that still produces a very satisfactory result.

Although this concentration and single focus can be effective in employment, it is often not the case in relationships. Yes, it works well if he is doing a job in the house, and his family is sure to get a first-class result. But it is sometimes this single focus that can cause havoc in communication and social interaction. Yet it can offer many advantages in family life. One man suggested that his ability to focus gave him the power to concentrate on complex issues and stay with these issues for hours. He said this gave him tremendous patience with his partner and the children when he was interacting with them or showing them how something worked.

Quite a few of the men I spoke to felt this ability to concentrate and focus was a great advantage of having Asperger syndrome. One man talked about how he had noticed that when things became unpleasant or uncomfortable, other people would back out and not be able to see things through to fruition. He felt he was able to see things through no matter how difficult or unpleasant it became for him. This appears to be a very strongly recognized characteristic of Asperger syndrome, which most of the men I spoke to were aware of.

It has been said, if you want a job of work done properly, ask a tradesman with Asperger syndrome, the job will be completed perfectly. One woman's husband decided to build her built-in wardrobes; she ended up with a perfect job, but it took him two years to complete.

Another advantage was that it had been a great benefit when studying particular subjects, and the subjects most named were the sciences. This, coupled with an ability to stick at the subject and maintain a focus no matter how unpleasant it seems, is certainly a great advantage within academic subjects and universities. Universities can be very safe places for someone with Asperger syndrome. Universities are about learning and academic issues, they are not about emotional openness and do not always involve having to be sociable, especially if the person is a mature student living at home. University studies also offer the perfect excuse not to socialize. Plausible reasons for not socializing could be having to work in the library or study for an exam or coursework. One may get labelled a boffin or a nerd, but it is more acceptable than in other environments and fields of work.

Another benefit suggested for AS was the ability to be objective. One AS man said that when his partner was becoming emotional over an issue and unable to cope with a problem that had presented itself, he could remain calm and sort things out. He would not become emotional or break down. Being objective and staying in control can be very useful and it is often a crisis that brings out these qualities in a person. One woman described how, when on holiday, she and her family had been travelling on a very lonely mountain road and came across a car that had skidded and overturned. It was dangerously near the edge, there was a strong smell of petrol and the engine was still running.

Her husband stopped their car and told his wife and children to remain in their seats. He ran up to the car that had crashed, managed to open one of the doors, turned off the engine and pulled out the lady driver and her two children. He carried the children to a safe place and then helped their mother. They were shaken up, not seriously injured. Soon after, another car arrived and the driver volunteered to take them to the local hospital. He got back in his car and never said a word, his wife was amazed at the brave and calm way he had dealt with what could have been a very tragic event. He carried on with their journey as though nothing unusual had happened. The most surprising thing of all was that when they arrived home he never related the tale of his bravery to anyone. When she asked him why not, he said he was just doing what anyone would do. I am sure many men would have done what he did, but most would have a wanted a little bit of glory for what they had so altruistically achieved.

This part of Asperger syndrome is not proud or conceited; it is modest and quite humble. The AS adult displays no need to tell people about the good and often gallant deeds that he has done. I can imagine that there are many unsung heroes out there who have Asperger syndrome!

The final advantage of having Asperger syndrome quoted by both partners was that it provided a reason for most of the problems in the relationship. Having a reason can make the difference as to whether the relationship survives or not. Some men decide they have Asperger syndrome through self-diagnosis and this is as far as they need to take it. Others may want to make it official and seek out a diagnosis. Whichever route is taken my research shows that in the majority of cases awareness of the syndrome is a benefit to both partners in the relationship. But,

although awareness can help the adult with AS develop a better understanding of some of the problems he has been experiencing it does not
always automatically make him feel better about himself.

Key points

- The majority of AS adults feel there are no benefits to
  having AS.
- The ability to concentrate and focus is offered as the
  greatest advantage of having AS.
- Another advantage is the ability to adhere to and
  maintain a focus while studying a particular subject.
- Being objective was also offered as an advantage.
- There could be many unknown and silent heroes with
  AS.

Conclusion

One man in my research questioned whether having Asperger syndrome set him apart from the rest of the human race. Another man who had recently been diagnosed with Asperger syndrome asked if that meant he no longer qualified as a 'normal' human being. These questions are profound and thought-provoking and echo accurately how many people with Asperger syndrome are often left feeling.

AS is not a madness or mental illness; it is a developmental disorder that is present from birth. If the individual with Asperger syndrome were born into a world where everyone had AS, he would not feel out of place or even be aware that he had a disability or that there were some things he could not do. He would not need social skills and would not need insightful thought because it would not be required or expected; it would be a skill that no one would have.

In other words, he would not have a problem at all. He would have the intelligence to find a job and this would not depend upon his social skills in the interview stage. He would be quite capable of looking after himself and maintaining his needs. He would only have to worry about the practical and logical problems in life. He would not have to offer emotional support, he would not have to mind-read, and he would not have to work out double meanings or sarcasm, because everyone on the planet would say what he means and mean what he said.

Looking at Asperger syndrome from this perspective shows clearly that the only problems the individual with Asperger syndrome has is getting on with, understanding and being accepted by people who do not have AS. It is only when the individual with Asperger syndrome tries to form relationships that the problems AS causes become apparent. Take away any human relationship and it is likely that the person with Asperger syndrome would be totally unaware that he has any problems. So the core problems are relationships, whether it is with school friends, work colleagues, the family, parents, children or partners.

It is from early social interaction that the AS individual begins to learn that he is different from the people around him. Constant rejection and bullying as a child can soon get the message across that there may be something wrong. It is sometimes not until the AS adult forms an intimate relationship that the subject of Asperger syndrome is raised, often by his partner. Once the individual is made aware that he possibly has Asperger syndrome, or when he is diagnosed, he has to make a choice. He has to decide if he is going to accept that he has Asperger syndrome, and understand the disorder and the effect it is having on him and those around him. Or he can completely deny it and look to blame his partner, family or society in general.

If he decides to be aware, then the relationship has a hope, especially if both partners are fully accepting and have willingness to work together. The problems in the relationship will not be automatically solved, but they can certainly be improved and some can be avoided in the future. It takes teamwork between the couple to make any relationship work, but this is especially true in a relationship affected by Asperger syndrome. Support for the couple and the whole family is essential. When an individual is diagnosed with AS, it is a family affair and all the members of the family will need to be aware and educated about this different way of being.

If, however, the person with Asperger syndrome is in denial and refuses to accept that he has the condition or is having any difficulties; if he blames his partner or his children, and they are made to suffer as a consequence, then the NT partner has a choice and that choice is to stay or to go. No one should be made to suffer in a relationship whether this is caused by financial, emotional, sexual, verbal or physical abuse,

A woman gave me a poem. She was living in a very unhappy relationship with a man with Asperger syndrome. He was in total denial of the problems he had and blamed her for everything. She wrote:

I am sitting on a precipice swaying to and fro
Should I jump?
Should I scream?
Or is it time to go?

The desperate level this woman had reached was obvious by what she wrote, and had she jumped she would have left behind four wonderful children. She did not jump as she recognized she had choices, she had tried screaming but there was no one to hear her or understand, so in the end she left.

Both partners in a relationship have a choice, the children do not have a choice and it is every parent's responsibility to see that their needs are taken into account. People have a responsibility both to themselves and to those around them. This responsibility does not diminish because a person has Asperger syndrome. Every individual and every couple experience will be different; I have brought to you just a glimpse into the lives of a collection of couples coping with Asperger syndrome.

It has been debated by professionals as to whether Asperger syndrome is a difference rather than a disability, I would say it is a different way of thinking that becomes a disability when interaction with others is required. This interaction may be at different levels, for some it is social interaction at any level, for others it is only when the relationship is an intimate couple relationship, or one that involves children.

Individuals with Asperger syndrome have much to offer and play an important role in our society. Their amazing capacity to focus, ability to achieve and the potential in some for superior intelligence has been responsible for many of the commodities we enjoy today.

In the introduction to this book it was asked whether the man with Asperger syndrome could love his partner? The answer is yes. He may show his love in a different way and his feelings will not always be obvious, but most men would argue that they do indeed love their partners. 'Do you love your partner?' is a question I ask many times in the counselling room. The answer I normally receive back from the AS partner is a rather surprised and straightforward, 'Yes of course I do!' No ribbons or bows, just the facts, thought out in a practical logical way.

His love for her is honest and enduring. He will never let her drown in the sea of emotions; he will jump in and rescue her before she even gets her feet wet. He will keep her safe and her feet firmly on the ground; he will look after her to the best of his ability. One man said, 'My wife is the only woman I have ever loved, I cannot imagine ever being with anyone else.' He meant what he said with all the sincerity he could offer, he could not indeed ever *imagine* being with someone else.

In relationships AS men are often very honest, loyal and hardworking, most will be faithful and remain with their chosen partner for life. They will give and offer love in the ways that they can. If their partners understand Asperger syndrome they will appreciate that this giving will often take a practical and active form. It is unlikely that an AS man will be able to offer emotional support or empathetic feelings. Some women will not be able to live with the emptiness and loneliness that this can bring.

Maybe John Gray should add a component to his book *Men are from Mars and Women are from Venus,* maybe he should add that AS individuals are from Saturn. All adults with Asperger syndrome are different as individuals but they all clearly come from the same planet and should be given the respect and support that would be offered to others coming from a different culture.

I would like to end this book with a quote from a man with Asperger syndrome. It is a statement that says clearly that it is time our society took Asperger syndrome more seriously and realized the pain that our ignorance is causing the thousands of adults and families affected by this socially inhibiting disorder.

> I wish I could have my brain rewired…so that I could feel like a normal fully paid up member of the human race, instead of a mentally dejected alien being!

Key points

- It is often when the AS adult tries to form relationships with others that having AS becomes a major problem.
- Awareness of AS offers a choice to both partners.
- Denial of AS can be destructive in a relationship.
- In relationships the majority of AS men are honest, faithful and hardworking.
- The AS adult is capable of loving his partner.

Frequently Asked Questions

I have divided this into three sections. The first section will cover questions asked by the partner who has Asperger syndrome, the second questions asked by their partner and the third questions asked by their children and in-laws.

Section 1 – Questions asked by the AS partner

Question 1 I have read that having AS means I cannot show empathy. I believe I do empathize with those around me, so is this true?

According to the Collins Dictionary empathy means 'the power of understanding and imaginatively entering into another person's feeling'. This is the true meaning of empathy and hence the answer to the question, 'Can people with Asperger syndrome empathize with others' is 'no'. So why is it that many people with AS believe they can empathize? Having Asperger syndrome does not equate to having no feelings and it does not mean being unable to recall those feelings and apply them to someone else in a situation that the AS adult perceives to be similar to the one he was once in. These feelings though, will be based purely on the AS person's memory of how he felt, he will not be able to connect with or imagine the feelings of the other person.

For example: A man who had been diagnosed with AS came to see me with his wife. During our consultation, the subject of empathy was raised and he argued that, despite what his wife said, he was able to empathize with her. I asked if he could describe a time when he had been able to do this. He offered a recent example of when her mother had been rushed into hospital after having a stroke, he said his wife was very stressed over this and he was able to understand how she was feeling. I asked him how he thought she felt and he replied that she must have been very upset by it. He then described the time when his father had been suddenly taken ill and rushed to hospital; he could remember how inconvenient and upsetting it was when a parent was unexpectedly taken ill.

His wife at this point said if he had understood he would not have been so insensitive towards her. He argued that he had only been trying to help her to carry on with her daily life. His wife explained that she had been desperately upset by what had happened and that she had felt unable to cope with everyday chores. He had suggested to her that she should refrain from going on about her mother and give more thought to looking after the house and getting the dinner ready.

It transpired that when his father was suddenly taken ill, he had dealt with it in a very logical way and had focused on the practical issues of keeping his father's business on track. He believed her feelings to be the same as his own and so, without realizing how damaging his comments were, he caused his wife distress.

He had believed he was empathizing with her and believed she would benefit from getting on with the household jobs, rather than talking about her concerns for her mum. He was, though, basing this on his own experience not hers. This is an area that I spend a lot of time working on with couples and I often use the analogy that, even though they may be standing on the same mountain, they are looking in different directions and feeling very differently about what they are seeing, experiencing and feeling.

Question 2 Why can't my partner just tell me what she wants me to do?

This is a question I hear so often from men with Aspergers. They say that if their partners would just tell them what they wanted, then they would be able to do this for them. To this comment the NT partner will often reply that it does not feel natural to have to voice her thoughts and if he loved her he would automatically know what she wanted. The ability to read her emotional state and guess what she wants is not automatic or even available to adults with AS and unless she is prepared to verbalize what she wants, then it is unlikely that he will know that is required or desired.

Having AS means that he is not able to mind-read and offer emotional responses to his partner in the way that is automatically available to most NT people. Because of the constant failures to get it right, the AS partner will be even less likely to attempt to guess what he is supposed to say or do as time goes by. To him, it seems so simple to rectify this problem and he will find it difficult to understand why she is reluctant to offer him the information he needs.

If the NT partner does not tell him how she feels and what she wants from him, it will result in a constant breakdown in communication between them and both will end up feeling hurt and resentful. It is difficult for the NT partner to adapt her interaction with him into this format and still believe that it is not because he does not care about her feelings. It may take time for her to adopt this new way of communicating, but it is vital if the relationship is going to work and it is certainly worth the effort as it will help avoid the feeling of being unheard, acknowledged and not valued. So the golden edict for the NT partner is, 'say what you mean and mean what you say'.

Question 3 My wife was affectionate towards me in bed and then became quite hostile when I tried to make love to her, why?

Having Asperger syndrome can make it very difficult to read the non-verbal signals given out by partners or to put things into context. A woman may be affectionate for a number of reasons; it may be that she has the feeling of being insecure, unloved, or it may be because she wants to feel close to her partner. It does not automatically mean she wants sex. It is very important that the couple find a way that she can let him know if she wants him to make love to her. Maybe they can negotiate a way in which she responds to him, whether that is in a sexual way that she touches him or by openly voicing what she wants to eliminate the possibility of getting it wrong. It would, over time, become part of the love making process and could help to improve this intimate act, as it would remove the fear of getting it wrong.

It can feel difficult to be more open and verbal in the lovemaking process, as sex is sometimes the one thing in the relationship that does not get discussed by the couple. She may find it difficult to say what she wants within the context of the bedroom, but it does get easier with practice.

Question 4 My wife's moods seems to change completely once a month and she becomes very angry and hostile towards me. Why?

What this man is describing is premenstrual tension (PMT) and this is an aspect of women that many men find difficult to comprehend or manage. To a man with AS, it can feel like a monthly personal attack on him that can result in the woman being permanently labelled as hostile, vindictive and angry. What it is like to be premenstrual and the havoc hormones can play with emotions is difficult for an AS man to put into context. For him, the inconsistency in her moods is very difficult to predict and due to the heightened sensitivity to criticism that can affect an adult with AS, it may be perceived that PMT is just an excuse to attack. The AS man will often focus only on his partner's moods and how she responds to him, he is unlikely to rationalize that it is about PMT and not about him.

Some couples keep a diary so he can be forewarned as to when she is likely to be in the premenstrual stage. If he can learn more about the female body, it may help his understanding. However, there was one case where a man learnt from a colleague that his colleague's wife did not experience PMT because she had had a hysterectomy. That night he suggested to his wife that she should have a hysterectomy too, as then she would be less of an angry person. She did indeed become quite angry at his suggestion and accused him of being very selfish.

Sometimes, if a third party explains the effects of PMT to him, it can be better understood and will be easier for him to accept. It is important too that the woman is able to rationalize that the way she feels is due to PMT and not because her AS partner is doing anything particularly different. Perhaps she can agree not to discuss sensitive issues at this time of the month or has a close friend on which to vent her feelings. Physical exercise can also be an excellent way for her to decrease premenstrual tension.

Question 5 My partner is constantly criticizing me, I feel I can not do anything right for her. Why does she put me down all the time?

Many AS men complain that they are constantly put down and criticized by their partners. There is often a heightened sensitivity to any form of perceived criticism in adults with AS. This can make it extremely difficult for their partner to challenge them, advise them or just try to be their friend. The woman can end up feeling exhausted and tired from being constantly accused of attacking her partner when she is often only trying to help.

Communication is the core issue here; it is so often the case that the message has been misinterpreted by the person receiving it and this causes a reaction rather than a response to what has been said. Working to improve communication is vital in AS relationships as it requires a completely different way of talking and hearing. It takes time and practice to achieve, but the effort taken pales in significance when weighed against the results that are gained.

Just using 'I' instead of 'you' can make a tremendous difference. The 'you' word can seem very accusatory and statements like, 'You need to do something about the way you behave when we go out,' can sound like a criticism and an attack. If the same statement is offered as, 'I know you try your hardest, but I am concerned that people will misunderstand your intentions when you don't shake their hands,' can sound much better.

For the AS adult it can be difficult to put things in context and he may only hear part of what has been said, which is why the choice of words and how much information is given in any one sentence is very important. Communicating in a different way can be achieved between the couple if both are committed to the relationship and have the mindset and energy to make it work. I have written more on strategies for improving communication in *The Other Half of Asperger Syndrome.*

Question 6 Why do my young children never seem to want me to spend time with them?

Imaginative play and games that involve making a fool of oneself can seem almost impossible for the adult with AS. Being able to play on a child's level means being able to understand the child's mind and the stage of development they are at. AS adults cannot do this and they are therefore more inclined to talk to and treat their children like adults. The children will sense this and may make remarks like 'Daddy's not fun to play with' or 'We want Mommy to play with us, not daddy!' This can hurt the AS adult who, although he will be aware it is difficult for him to join in with the kids, will feel that he has been doing his best. This can cause him to withdraw altogether and no longer participate in the children's games.

It is important to try to find things that both father and child can enjoy, it may be reading together, riding a bike or just sharing a chore together. Children need to feel the parent wants to participate in some part of their lives and if any common ground can be found between the child and the AS parent, it needs to be worked on and developed. For instance, one teenage boy said he was really proud of his dad because every time they had a family quiz evening at the school, his dad won it.

Question 7 Why does my wife always accuse me of not listening to what she says, when I am sure it is because she has not told me in the first place?

Adults with Asperger syndrome can have a very selective memory. This may be the result of distraction or, if the conversation is about feelings and emotions, it is unlikely he will have properly understood the content and therefore all the messages will not have been retained.

When the problem has been caused by distraction, it is because the AS adult has difficulty dealing with more than one issue or subject at a time. If there are lots of things going on when the message is being given, he can easily miss much of what is being said. All too often, there is a lot going on in the family home and is should be a consideration that, if possible, important messages should be timed for quiet moments.

The other reason he may not have heard the message that was given is because of the content of the conversation. Conversations about emotions and feeling are often given in an abstract and ambiguous way. This can be confusing for the partner with AS unless the message is translated into a language that he can understand. This language is concrete and logical and as long as it is delivered in a calm atmosphere it will be heard and understood. A new way of talking is often the only way forward.

Section 2 – Questions asked by the NT partner

Question 1 My partner went for a diagnosis and was told he only had autistic traits. What does this mean?

Some adults with Asperger syndrome who have been for a diagnosis have been told they do not have Asperger syndrome, but do have autistic traits.

The result can be that they leave the consultation room not fully under-standing what this means and its implications.

First, it needs to said that, whatever the result is of a diagnosis, it is only ever the opinion of the person making the diagnosis and how they use the particular criteria and given information available to them for diagnosis. The professionals' knowledge and familiarity of Asperger syndrome will affect the diagnosis. Such variables as whether they are more familiar with autism than Asperger syndrome or whether they work with adults with AS or children, can make a difference to their awareness.

The type of questions that are asked and how they are asked can also affect the diagnosis. As an example, many adults with AS when asked if they had any friends as children will answer 'Yes'. Sometimes, though, the reality of this is quite different and the AS individual's perception of 'friend' must be checked closely.

Something else that may affect diagnosis is how able the AS person has become over the years in disguising the more obvious signs of AS. Some AS adults have reported working very hard on developing their social abilities and are quite able for a limited period of time to keep up a good display of social skills, such as eye contact and body language. This is very difficult for them to maintain for long periods of time, but the interview process is rarely over three hours and in some respects many of the questions are predictable, especially if the AS person is well informed about the difficulties AS can cause. The professional making the diagnosis needs to take this into account. That is why, if the AS adult is in a long-term relationship, it is essential that he takes his partner along to take an active part in the process. The partner often knows him better than any one else and in the adult stage of his life, often better than his parents.

In some cases it is requested that the parents are present at the diagnosis and this is ideal if the AS person is a child or young adult, but not if he is an older adult and has been in a long-term relationship. The parents' memories will be retrospective and may be unintentionally biased, parents will not want to be told that their grown-up child has Asperger syndrome. This might leave them with feelings of guilt that they let their child down by not being aware that the problems their child was experiencing were, in fact, due AS. I know of cases when this has happened and the eventual diagnosis was swayed by some of the answers given by the parents. The answers given by the parents were not always accurate and the eventual diagnosis given has been one of autistic traits. The effect this can have on the adult with Asperger syndrome can be devastating and could leave them feeling like a fake. In one case where this happened the man later went for a second opinion with his partner and was told that he clearly had Asperger syndrome. Only then did he feel validated and no longer responsible for the difficulties he had been having in his role as a husband and father.

I would recommend to anyone having a diagnosis to seek out a second opinion if they are not entirely happy with it. It would be very unusual for some one who had self-diagnosed to be wrong. It is though, much more likely that it will be the NT partner who detects the presence of AS and it is equally likely that there will be some strong support to her hypothesis.

Question 2 Now he is aware he has AS will he be able to change?

Whether or not the AS partner will make the effort to change is dependent on a number of factors. The most important is probably whether he actually accepts the diagnosis and the fact that there are things about himself that need to be changed for the sake of the relationship. Acceptance of the diagnosis is paramount to possible change. I have encountered some adults who know they have AS but refuse to accept it, often because they feel it would damage their perception about themselves. It may also mean that they will have to take responsibility for some of the problems in the relationship and accept that there are some things they cannot do. It is the relationships in which AS is denied that are more likely to break down, because the AS partner is likely to externalize the blame. Very often this is onto the NT partner who will possibly be banned from even mentioning the words Asperger syndrome.

So the answer to the question is yes, he can make some changes, but only if the partner accepts he has AS, is aware of its debilitating factors and develops an understanding of the condition. If this happens he is more likely to be able to make some changes to the way he is behaving and learn to understand his partner and his partner's needs more accurately.

Question 3 Can medication help alleviate the symptoms of Asperger syndrome?

The likelihood of anxiety and depression is higher in cases of Asperger syndrome than in control groups. Anti-depressants have shown in some cases to be successful in controlling anxiety and alleviating stress. They will not make any difference to the core symptoms of Asperger syndrome, but they may alleviate the anxiety, stress and sometimes depression that can be a consequence of having AS. This is not surprising when one considers the pressure that society places upon the individual to be acceptable and efficient in communication and interaction.

Some AS adults find the idea of taking medication abhorrent and they are very suspicious of the affect it will have on them. This may be based on a prior experience when medication has not worked for them or it may be a message carried down from the family background. This will be very incapacitating and difficult to change; in some cases it could cause even more anxiety and stress for the AS adult if they feel pressured into taking medication.

Question 4 Why are men more affected than women?

I am coming into contact with more and more women with Asperger syndrome. I am also aware that women are often far harder to detect than men. Women with AS do try very hard to be perceived as 'normal' and often work very hard to achieve this.

At the turn of century the AS male may have been regarded as just behaving like a man. The more subtle signs of the condition may have been overlooked or just regarded as odd or eccentric. One of the reasons it may now appear that AS is on the increase in men is possibly the way women are now challenging this distant and unattached behaviour. In the past, women would not have been able to do this. Women in relationships now have more rights and are able to make more demands on their partners; they are not as dependent on their partners and feel able to question his behaviour. Consequently, it is often the NT partner that recognizes that Asperger syndrome may be affecting the relationship.

It is possible that as more knowledge comes to light, men will likewise start to recognize it in their female partners. In my research, all the AS women I came into contact with were in relationships with men who were also on the autistic spectrum and in all cases it had been the woman who had become aware of AS in herself. Had her partner not been on the autistic spectrum we do not know whether he would have come to realize that she had AS.

Women with AS are far more able to disguise the problems and difficulties it causes and do seem to make far more effort to do this. So although Asperger syndrome appears to affect more men than women, the difference may not be a vast as is currently thought.

Question 5 When I described my husband's behaviour to a friend, she said he was simply being a 'male'. Is she right?

Many of the women who have come to see me for counselling describe a time when they were told by a friend or confidante that their partner's behaviour was no different to that of any other man. They were told that their partner is simply being male! Comments like this can be very damaging and cause the NT partner to feel she is judging her partner too strongly, or that her expectations for emotional support in the relationship are over demanding. This could not be further from the truth; the expectations they have are not extreme and would be within the capabilities of most men who did not have Asperger syndrome.

The largest difference between men with Asperger syndrome and men who do not is choice. The NT man can choose to emotionally support his partner, he can take on more responsibility for the relationship and he can empathize with her feelings. The AS man does not have this choice and cannot do these things, he simply does not have the ability. It is a case of cannot do rather than will not do. This is one of the positives in discovering AS is the cause of some of the problems. The NT women now knows that her partner is not being selfish or vindictive towards her. She was accurate in her assumptions that something deeper was wrong and it was not because she was losing her sanity.

Question 6 My husband has been diagnosed with AS but does not have any particular obsessions.

Having obsessive tendencies is seen as one of the criteria of Asperger syndrome and yet many couples report that there are no obvious obsessive tendencies or special interests held by the AS partner. When I am told of this, I often dig deeper. I may first ask about his profession and discover that he spends as much time as he can at work. I may then discover that he works in computers or that he is an engineer. One man I encountered was a train driver and knew everything he could know about trains. His family had not regarded this as an obsession because it was his work but in fact it was his obsession and had become his chosen career. It is sometimes presumed that the obsession or special interest of an AS person would have to be odd or unusual. This is not always the case and with so many varied opportunities in careers today, it is not unusual for the choice of work to be the special interest.

In other cases, I have found the obsession may be watching the television or doing the gardening, neither of these appear unusual, but if they were suddenly restricted or denied to the AS adult then stress and anxiety might increase. This is quite usual in the case of obsessive behaviour.

Question 7 I have read that men with AS are not very good at dealing with the financial side of the relationship. My husband deals with all the bills and accounts and does it very well. Is he different from other men with his condition?

No, he is not different he just has an ability rather than a disability in this area. I have found that there seem to be very few shades of grey in adults with AS and it appears to cause complete opposites in some of the types of behaviour displayed. It can seem as though AS adults are polarized at either end of the scale and there is an either/or situation. For instance, some men with AS are immaculate in their appearance, their choice of clothes and personal hygiene. Others have no dress sense whatsoever and do not appear to be bothered by their appearance or, in some cases, their bodily cleanliness. Some AS men are fanatical about time and would never be late, while others have no concept of time and are always running behind schedule. This polar opposite can be applied to many aspects of life, which also includes the ability to handle financial issues.

No one is completely certain why this phenomenon seems to be apparent in AS and it does add confusion to anyone trying to assess if a person has Asperger syndrome. This is very apparent when the NT adult describes her partner's behaviour and habits to another in the same situation who then describes her AS partner as being completely opposite. What does seem apparent is that AS has the capability to take the individual's natural traits and exaggerate them. So if the adult had the ability to be good with monetary matters, then having Asperger syndrome may exaggerate this trait and his ability may seem to verge on perfectionism.

Question 8 My partner spends all his time on the computer; he stays up late and does not spend time with me. I feel he prefers the computer to me. Is there any way I can stop this?

Computers and AS can be very compatible and when the Internet is added, it can feel like a safe place for the AS man to explore. He can gain information and research his interests without having to talk face to face with another person or leave the safety of his office or study. The Internet can provide him with all the information he needs on his special interest and emails are often his preferred way of communicating.

The AS person though, can have the tendency to become obsessive about being on the computer and not have the desire to do much else. Like listening to music or watching the television, it enables him to focus on one particular thing and switch everything else off. It is for him a form of relaxing. It is important for the NT partner to negotiate and compromise the time spent on the computer before it becomes too obsessive. It would have to be a form of compromise he understood and that made sense to him. It would be pointless saying he could not spend time on the computer because you wanted him to watch television with you instead.

His logic would ask why was he not allowed to sit in front of one screen, but told to sit in front of another. He would need to understand that you wanted him to be with you spending quality time together. This quality time may be walking the dog together or pursuing a favourite activity, maybe spending time with the children, or helping them with their homework. He is able to negotiate and understand reason if it is put to him in a way that makes logical sense.

Question 9 I have discovered my husband has been spending time on the porn channel on the Internet, but when I challenged him, he had no concept of the pain it caused me. How can this be when he knows that I want to keep this part of our relationship exclusive?

The availability of porn on the Internet is beginning to present more and more problems in relationships, irrespective of whether one partner has AS. The Internet brings sex and the availability of sex right into our homes. In the past, if a person wanted to look at porn or contact an available woman, he would have to look for it, either in contact magazines, sex shops or red light areas. This is no longer the case and sex is now available at the click of a button.

Quite a few AS men I have spoken to have expressed an almost adolescent curiosity in women and sex. Most have had very few and often only one sexual partner. Some are in a relationship where sex does not take place and they have chosen celibacy or self-gratification in the form of masturbation. The porn channels can appear to be an ideal way for them to explore and discover more about sex without the human contact.

When the NT partner discovers what he has been doing, the AS adult's reaction will often be one of complete justification that his actions have not harmed anyone and he has not been unfaithful. He may show a complete lack of remorse or any awareness that his actions would have caused so much pain and anger.

This is due to not being able to see things from his partner's perspective; he will only see things from his own perspective. If he looked at the porn through curiosity and never thought about being unfaithful or taking it further, he will expect his partner to understand this and not be threatened by it. Also, if it had not been clarified earlier in the relationship that this was something he was not allowed to do, he may have felt that it was therefore acceptable.

Rules and boundaries have to be very carefully discussed and decided upon by the couple; it can never be presumed that unspoken rules will be automatically followed. If the AS man has already become obsessive about Internet porn, he must realize that if he continues in his obsession the relationship with his partner might end. He will then have to decide what is more important to him, his relationship with his partner or spending time on the porn channels.

Question 10 Why is it he can manage a responsible job, yet I am unable to trust him to look after the children?

This is what makes AS such a paradox and confuses so many people. The AS adult is often very competent and efficient within his area of work and in dealing with practical and logical tasks that are easy to predict. Unfortunately, children are not practical or logical and they are certainly not predictable.

It is important to remember that Aspergers syndrome does not affect the intellectual part of the brain or the part of the brain that uses logic. It does though have a debilitating affect on the social segment of the brain, the parts of the brain that can mind-read and automatically understand another's mental state from the signals it is given. Looking after children requires many skills that for most NT adults are quite automatic and they just 'know' what to do in different situations. Adults with AS often need instructions or information on what to do, especially if the unexpected happens.

The other area that may make it difficult for him when looking after the children is distraction. Distraction can play a major disruptive role in the lives of some AS adults. The distraction may just be the television; if something of interest comes on the AS adult may become totally absorbed in what he is watching and temporarily forget the children in his charge. This can be potentially dangerous if, for example, a small child is left alone in the bath or near the source of power or heat. Fortunately, most of the time distraction does not pose a problem, but if something goes wrong, he may find his partner will not trust him again.

Question 11 My husband did not want children and I feel he has never forgiven me for becoming pregnant and having his child. My daughter is now twenty and it has never been a good relationship between them. Does he bear a grudge?

Unfortunately, he probably does. Some AS men can be quite bitter and vindictive if they truly believe they have in some way been wronged or deceived. This animosity can be life-long and will be directed towards the person who they perceived wronged them. Unfortunately, it is often out of context and totally unjustified. The AS man who instigated this question has not been able to weigh up the benefits he has received from having a child; his focus is only on the fact that his wife, in his eyes, deceived him into getting her pregnant. He has also not been able to understand that within the realms of marriage or cohabitation it is not unusual for a couple to have a child. He can only see what happened as a deceitful act and blame her entirely for this. His interaction with his daughter will have been grudged because he will see her as a constant reminder of his wife's deceit. He may also detach himself from his daughter because he considers her to be his wife's responsibility and will take opportunities to pay his wife back by not participating in the care and upbringing of their child. It is very sad when this happens because it is disruptive for the whole family and may have long-term damaging effects on his daughter.

Question 12 My husband refused to go to his son's graduation, because he had a meeting at work. How can he be so selfish?

Sometimes having AS can inhibit those affected from understanding what is expected of them and that their presence is important to their family. The AS man's rationale behind this case may be that his son's mother and grandparents were going so there was no need for him to be there as well. He might also feel that when he goes out with the family, they always seem to point out something wrong that he has said or done so he might be avoiding the situation.

Another important reason why he may avoid going is because graduations and similar events are very large social gatherings. Large social gatherings can be very difficult for people with AS. It is important to check out what the reasons are behind the AS parent's decision as it might not always be the way it appears, which is often total selfishness.

Question 13 My husband does not get on with his in-laws and refuses to even try. I feel as though I am stuck in the middle. Is there any way I can improve the situation?

Adults with AS have been known to show an intense dislike to some family members and to be very rude and hostile. This man will have in his perception, a logical and justified reason for not getting on with or liking his in-laws. It may be something he overheard them say and misinterpreted. He may feel threatened by them and think that they will turn their daughter against him. There will be a reason, but he may not want to say what it is. This can make it very difficult to sort out and it could be worth seeking outside help from a counsellor or an unbiased third party. If he feels he will be understood and his reasons will not be minimized or cause an argument he may be more likely to verbalize what the issue is.

If it cannot be resolved and his rude behaviour continues, then the NT partner may have to decide either to see her parents in his absence or to turn a blind eye to his behaviour.

Question 14 My partner can be very verbally abusive to me when I am only trying to help him. Why?

Verbal abuse in couple relationships can have a detrimental affect on the partners' self-esteem. In some instances the AS adult may react to his partner in a verbally abusive way for what might feel like an unwarranted attack. This untimely reaction can be due to how he has interpreted a specific situation. It is often because he has misinterpreted the meaning of what has been said to him by his partner. For example, she may simply have mentioned that the tap still needs fixing and, as she realizes how busy he is, she has asked her brother if he would do it for them. His interpretation of this may be that she is accusing him of being lazy or thoughtless or that he has let her down and she thinks he is inferior to every other man. To this he may react with instant anger, asking her why she does not go and live with her brother as she thinks he is so wonderful. He may continue to tell her that she is always attacking him and putting him down to get her own way. His reaction to her will be out of context, extreme and seem very cruel. She will feel very hurt and abused by his words and probably end up apologizing. This example may seem like an exaggeration but it is a very realistic situation when one partner has Asperger syndrome.

He will be feeling defensive and honestly believe that she is attacking and putting him down. He will feel justified in what he said and his reaction and believe that he was just standing up for himself. If she had actually been attacking him, there might be some justification for his verbal reaction, but as this was not her intention, it will feel very unjustified. He will not be able to see that her intent was not as he perceived it to be. He will not be able to put himself in his partner's shoes and realize that she was trying to help him and appreciate that she was trying to save him the bother of fixing the tap. This is an example of the type of issue that I spend time working on in the counselling room. Irrespective of the nature of the subject the fundamental issue is that both have to learn to talk to each other in a way that they can both interpret correctly.

However, sometimes the AS partner can be intentionally verbally abusive and this manner of treating his partner can become a habit. It may also be that she is verbally abusive to him. Verbal abuse is destructive and has a very negative effect on the self-esteem of both partners. It achieves absolutely nothing and if left unresolved will have a destructive effect on the relationship and could be damaging if there are children involved. They may eventually have to decide if they are going to continue this relationship with this pattern of verbal abuse.

Question 15 My partner has Asperger syndrome. Does this increase the likelihood that he will become violent towards me?

Forty per cent of the AS adults who took part in the research for this book reported that, at some time in the relationship, they had been physically abusive towards their partners. This is twice as high as the reported national average of twenty per cent. In all but two cases the violence was minimal and not classified by either partner as severe. The definition of severe violence would be hitting, slapping, punching, kicking, stabbing, breaking skin, throwing the person and using any form of weapon against them. Minimal violence, as referred to in this research, would be shoving, pushing or restraining. Thirty per cent of the AS men in my research reported that their reaction was either in self-defence or to restrain their partners and these occurrences were quite rare. Sometimes, the violence was a consequence of frustration and losing control.

Staying in control appears to be essential to the majority of AS men who work very hard to maintain control in their lives. In cases of violent behaviour, it is often a consequence of the AS man losing control of himself that provokes him into being physically aggressive, rather than him trying to control the other person. It is the latter that has a higher probability in recurring domestic violence.

The majority of violence reported was minimal in the sample of men who knew and accepted that they had AS. The story is very different for the AS men who denied they had the syndrome and blamed their partners for all the problems in the relationship. They did not show the same remorse for their behaviour and some felt that their partners had asked for the physical abuse that was directed towards them.

So to answer the question based on my own research, a man who has Asperger syndrome and accepts this fact is not more predisposed to be severely violent towards his partner than a NT male. If though, he is undiagnosed or refuses to accept the possibility that he may be affected by AS, the violence is more likely to be severe and recurring.

Question 16 My husband refuses to have any sexual contact with me whatsoever. Why?

The answer to this question may involve anger, lack of sexual desire or need and low self-esteem.

Suppressed anger is not unusual in cases of adults with Asperger syndrome and often the first thing to go is physical affection. The AS man may do this intentionally, particularly if it is something his partner has done that he is angry about and he knows that sex is something she wants from him. It is his way of silently saying he is not happy with something that is happening in the relationship. This can be very frustrating for the partner who will probably have no awareness of what she has done wrong.

Lack of sexual desire is another common reason why sex is withdrawn in AS relationships. This does not mean that the AS man does not have sexual needs or does not want to have an orgasm, it is more likely to mean that he does not want or need to share the experience with anyone else, including his partner. This can be quite complex and I talk more about these issues in Chapter 13.

Low self-esteem is another reason why the AS man may withdraw sexually, especially if his partner only tells him when he reads the signals wrong and does not tell him when he gets it right. Sex needs to be talked about, especially in AS relationships. He will not know what she wants from him and will often misinterpret what she is trying to convey. It is likely that he will be very sensitive to criticism and will became reluctant to even attempt to have sex for fear that he will get it wrong again. It can take a long time and much patience to eliminate these fears.

Question 17 My AS husband's mother died recently and he did not appear to grieve for her for very long. I still miss her very much, yet he never mentions her at all. Why is this?

The grieving process in adults with AS appears to be shorter than it is with NT adults and this is not indicative of how attached and close they were to the deceased person.

One reason for this may be the way that most AS adults deal with emotional problems, by using logic and working things out in a practical way. When an NT person loses a loved one, it is often the emotional bond that she shared with the deceased that is missed most. The deceased is also missed because of the practical role she played, perhaps the meals she cooked or how she helped with the shopping. These are practicalities that can be replaced. Replacing shared intimate chats or the mutual emotional support is far more difficult.

For the AS adult, the loss may be based more on practical issues and, as I have mentioned, these can be replaced more easily. It is unlikely that he would have shared an emotional dependence with the deceased, so as this type of emotional reliance was never formed it cannot be missed. This does not imply he did not love or care for the deceased person, it simply means that his love took a different form and was based on different needs than those of an NT person.

Another reason that has been put forward by an AS adult is that the mourning process by people with AS is displayed in a different way. The feelings of loss are the same, but the AS adult is more likely to internalize the sadness and mourning becomes a very private process.

Section 3 – Questions asked by the children and the in-laws.

Question 1 Why does my AS father never seem to appreciate me for who I am?

Many children with AS parents report feeling that they are only acknowledged by the AS parent for what they achieve or for serving a particular purpose. This can leave the child feeling unloved, not appreciated or not valued for who he is. Actions rather than feelings play an important role in the life of the AS parent, it is far easier for him to read people by their actions and the words they say than by their deeper feelings. If one of his offspring has achieved something concrete, then the AS parent will find this far easier to relate to and acknowledge than the fact that he is a kind person that likes to do nice things for others. The AS parent may not even appear to notice some of the finer qualities that his child displays and there will be times when his son or daughter might end up thinking that his or her efforts to be kind, considerate or thoughtful are completely wasted and begin to rebel instead.

It is sad when this happens and it is often because neither parent nor child is aware of AS and the effects it can have. Both are expecting something the other is not able to give, the child is quite rightly expecting unconditional positive support and love and the AS parent expects the child to be able to get along without it. There are no easy solutions to this problem, only to offer children the knowledge that their AS mum or dad is struggling to be a parent and often not even aware that he or she is not meeting their child's emotional needs.

Question 2 My father seems to hate all my friends but they are really OK. Why?

I have heard many accounts of how difficult the AS parent can make it for his children to bring their friends back to the house. Children, especially adolescents, describe their AS parents as being hostile, odd, silent, rude, offensive and sometimes just completely ignorant to their friends. If the family is not aware that the parent has AS, or the child does not want his friends to know about the AS parent, then it can be very difficult to explain to his friends why Dad is behaving in this way. His friends may even decide that they do not want to visit again.

Adolescence can be nightmare time in the AS family and rules and boundaries have to be put firmly in place. If the parent is aware that he has AS, then maybe some rules can be discussed with him. For example, if the problem is that the AS parent just stares at his children's friends without speaking it could be explained to him that it is not polite and he could try greeting them with a simple hello. It is difficult for the AS parent to make small talk and he is often at a complete loss as to what to say. His home will often be his safe place and it will feel threatening for him to find it filled with a load of strangers, that he neither knows nor invited. He may view his teenager's friends as being just as odd as they think he is. He may find their clothes, hair or language difficult to understand. The trouble is that he will show it, because he is not very good at hiding his feelings or thoughts. He will not be aware of how embarrassing or rude he is being, because he does not pick up other people's feelings of embarrassment.

There is no easy way to deal with this AS family problem and unfortunately it will be the child who will feel he or she is losing out and unable to entertain his or her friends. Perhaps friends could be asked to visit while the AS parent is at work or it could be explained to them that the parent has AS and the apparently rude behaviour is not intentional.

Question 3 Why is my AS mother so unpredictable in her emotions?

A lot of expectations are placed on a mother and one of them is being able to mind-read and know automatically what the rest of the family want and need from her. This can put tremendous pressure on the AS mum who is unlikely to be receiving any support from someone who understands her difficulties. It is likely that she will be struggling trying to fulfill her family's needs and, because she may not always show the stress she is feeling, it may appear that she is managing. Unfortunately, this will slowly wear her down until she snaps. It may be something quite small or irrelevant that will be the catalyst that makes her lose control and become either very angry or burst into tears.

Once the family is aware that mum has Asperger syndrome, they can work together and if the children are old enough, they can learn to take more responsibility for themselves instead of expecting mum to do everything. Once this is accepted, these apparent mood swings may desist. Some of the pressure has to be taken off her. If the family works together and develops a better understanding of what AS causes and the effects it can have on family life, then improvements can be achieved. This can take time and it is important that Mum is offered all the support she requires.

Question 4 Our son-in-law has been diagnosed with Asperger syndrome. Does this mean all our grandchildren will have it?

No, it does not mean they will have Asperger syndrome, but it does mean the likelihood of them having it is increased. There is evidence for a genetic cause in AS, but exactly how this works is not yet completely understood. It has been suggested that when one of the parents has Asperger syndrome, there is a one in three chance that a child of that parent will be also be on the autistic spectrum. Some parents though, may have all of the children affected by autism and others may have none affected at all. Time and research will hopefully come up with more answers to this question. The most important aspect at this stage is that parents are aware of the possibility that one or more of their children may be affected and can therefore spot the disorder quite early and provide as much support and help for the child that they possibly can. Early intervention does make a difference and, because intelligence is not affected by Asperger syndrome, it is possible for the child to learn to be more acceptable in society and learn some of the less obvious social rules.

Question 5 Our daughter has just told us that her fiancé has been diagnosed with Asperger syndrome. We have not got a clue what the implications of this disorder are. Do we need to be concerned about her?

It does not mean there is a need to be concerned about her; it does mean that, as part of an AS family, there will be a need for all members to be educated about and understand what it means to have Asperger syndrome.

Asperger syndrome is a very complex disorder and affects three core areas, communication, social interaction and imagination, producing narrow and repetitive interests. It is not a mental illness and is not catching. It is a developmental disorder and the individual will have difficulties in the three core areas mentioned. It will not affect intelligence or the individual's persona. There are nice people and nasty people and there are lots of in-between people. Having AS does not make someone nice or nasty, passive or aggressive, selfish or altruistic. It does, however, cause problems in communication that can develop into misunderstandings; it does prevent the person from being able to read the emotional state of another person and this alone can cause havoc in a family. It can exaggerate some of the person's characteristics, exacerbating some of his ways and habits and making these seem extreme.

What will make the biggest difference to the relationship is the basic personality of the person who has AS. The level of his awareness of Asperger syndrome, his acceptance of it and the difficulties he has, are just as important as the awareness and acceptance of the people who love him. My advice to anyone who has recently discovered that a loved one has Asperger syndrome is to read and learn as much about this complex disorder as possible.

Resources for Adults with Asperger Syndrome and their Families

Counselling and research

Maxine Aston BSc Hon Psychology. Couple Counselling Certificate Relate.

Author of *The Other Half of Asperger Syndrome* National Autistic Society (2000).

Works as a couple counsellor, specializing in couples and families affected by Asperger syndrome. Counselling has been found to be beneficial when Asperger syndrome is understood and accepted by both the couple and the couple counsellor.

I am currently writing a doctorate on Asperger syndrome and its effect on the couple relationship and the family. I would be pleased to hear from anyone who would be willing to fill in a questionnaire or, if geographically possible, be interviewed by me.

For counselling services or to participate in my research contact maxineaston@aol.com or visit my website www.maxineaston.co.uk.

Support Groups

I invited the owners of the following support groups to describe them in their own words. Here are their accounts:

ASpar

ASpar was founded in 1999 as a support group and information exchange for people raised by one or more parents with AS. The founder, Judy Singer, searched the whole world over to find a precedent for her uniquely dysfunctional family, through the psychiatric textbooks, through all kinds of expensive and mostly irrelevant therapy. As with so many in the AS community, it was when she realized that her own daughter had AS that the penny dropped that her mother's 'impossible' behaviour was not a bad moral choice, but a hereditary disability. Judy Singer states, 'Over the past three years the members of ASpar have shared their stories and a general picture is emerging of what we have in common. One of the most painful things to emerge has been the invalidation we recieved from the NT world and the helping professions. Our mission now is twofold. First to continue to support our members to tell their stories to others who really know what it is like, so that they can finally get it out of their system, and move on with their lives. And second to educate the public about the difficulties when AS parents' raise kids, so that there is no excuse for children to endure what we did. We do not want to say that all AS people are necessarily bad parents, but when they are it manifests in certain recognizable ways. Society needs to be aware and ready to put solid resources behind supporting AS affected families.' www.aspar.klattu.com.au

ASPIRES

Asperger Syndrome Partners and Individuals Resources Encouragement and Support.

ASPIRES is an on-line resource for spouses and family members of adults diagnosed or suspected to be on the autistic spectrum. Our approach toward one another, as well as our 'significant others', is directed towards solving spectrum-caused problems in our relationships in a positive and understanding manner. Through personal poetry, essays, and additionally published information, we attempt to positively educate all who are 'touched' by Asperger syndrome or Autism Spectrum Disabilities.

ASPIRES is also an e-mail subscription list for individuals with Asperger syndrome (AS) or high functioning autism, as well as those who have a parent, partner, spouse, or child with AS. We share our family and relational experience, resources, and survival tips as well as offering encouragement and hope. Through sharing, we hope to lighten one another's burdens and find positive solutions to many of the challenges that characterize our relationships. We are based on individual trust and confidence between members, and will not allow any professional or commercial use of our list. ASPIRES is international in membership and interests, but is limited to using English as its primary language. Our motto is 'We might not always agree, but together we will make a difference.' ASPIRES is accessed at: www.justgathertogether.com/aspires.html

FAAAS

FAAAS Inc. (Families of ADULTS Afflicted with Asperger's Syndrome) is a website and non-profit organization with a mission to bring awareness of Asperger syndrome in the ADULT population, to professionals, as well as to the public. FAAAS Inc. also offers families information and validation of this neurological/biological/medical disorder in adults, and how AS can and does affect the entire family unit...and beyond. Professionals in many different areas recognize that ASD is pandemic. These same professionals are ignoring the fact there are millions of families around the world, doing the best they can for their ADULT family members, who have never been diagnosed with ASD, but who ARE on the spectrum.

There is no support, no assistance, no validation for these families who struggle every day to do the best they can for their ADULT family member on the autistic spectrum.

Adults, who have had multiple difficulties in their lives, have contacted FAAAS, Inc. and have recognized THEIR lives as probably being AS, by reading the information posted to our website.

Many families recognize AS behaviours in an adult family member, only after a child has recently been diagnosed as having Asperger syndrome.

FAAAS Inc. is attempting to educate and inform the professionals, and the public about Asperger syndrome, especially AS in the adult population. FAAAS Inc. is accessed at: www.faaas.org

Families of Adults Afflicted with Asperger Syndrome
PO Box 514 Centerville
MA 0263
US

OASIS

Founded in 1995, this online resource provides the most comprehensive and up-to-date information to families of individuals with Asperger syndrome, adults with Asperger syndrome and professionals who work with them. At the website you will find descriptions of the diagnosis, information on educational interventions, listings of local, online and international support groups, listings of clinicians who treat AS, listings of conferences and workshops, and much more. In addition, OASIS sponsors two message board/chatroom forums where families will find immediate support. OASIS is not a nonprofit organization and there are no fees or membership dues required in order to participate in the forum or website.

The OASIS site and forum is a nonfunded volunteer effort. If OASIS has been helpful to you or your family and you would like to help, please visit www.aspergersyndrome.org/help_oasis.html

The *Oasis Guide To Asperger Syndrome* by Patricia Romanowski Bashe and Barbara L. Kirby (Crown, 2001) is now available. For reviews and information please visit www.aspergersyndrome.org/oasis_guide.html OASIS (Online Asperger Syndrome Information and Support) at www.aspergersyndrome.org/ information

Information

Asperger-marriage Website

Chris and Gisela Slater-Walker are the first married couple to offer readers an insight into living in a relationship when one partner has Asperger syndrome.

To find out more about their inspiring new book visit their website.www.asperger-marriage.info.

Dr. Tony Attwood

Leading authority on Asperger syndrome whose books and worldwide conferences have helped many people become aware and understand more about this disorder. His website is packed with information, latest research and news. www.tonyattwood.com

NAS (National Autistic Society)

Head Office
393 City Road,
London EC1V 1NG
Tel: 020 7833 2299
Fax: 020 7833 9666
Autism Helpline: 0870 600 8585
Lines open Monday to Friday, 10 a.m. until 4 p.m.
www.nas.org.uk

OAASIS

OAASIS (Office for Advice, Assistance, Support and Information on Special needs) is an information service for parents, teachers and others with an interest in special education, and in particular autism spectrum disorders. The Hesley Group, an independent company running ten residential special schools and colleges, established it in 1996. OAASIS runs a telephone Helpline (09068 633201 – calls cost 60p a minute), and produces a range of publications, from its free one-page OAASIS information sheets, to the 'First Guides' series of booklets for parents and teachers. All its information sheets are on the website. It acts as a point of information on all the Hesley Group schools and colleges and can also offer help on how to find other special schools and colleges, both independent and mainstream.

Brock House
Grigg Lane
Brockenhurst
Hampshire
SO42 7RE
UK
www.oaasis.co.uk

References

Aston, M.C. (2000) *The Other Half of Asperger Syndrome*. London: National Autistic Society.

Aston, M.C. and Forrester, R. (2002) 'Living with Asperger's.' *Community Care: Issue 1430* (11–17 July).

Attwood, T. (1998) *Asperger's Syndrome: A Guide for Parents and Professionals*. London: Jessica Kingsley Publishers.

Brown, G.W. (1993) 'The role of life events in the aetiology of depressive and anxiety disorders.' In S.D. Stanford and P. Salmon (eds). *Stress: From Synapse to Syndrome*. London: Academic Press, 3–50. In J. Herbert (1997). Fortnightly review: Stress, the Brian and Mental Illness. BMJ 315, 530-5.

Carter, R. (1998) *Mapping the Mind*. London: Weidenfeld & Nicolson.

Gray, J. (1992) *Men are from Mars, Women are from Venus*. New York: HarperCollins Publishers.

Henderson, L. and Hackett, N. (2002) 'Asperger's syndrome in child contact cases.' *Family Law*. (February).

Hester, M., Pearson, C. and Harwin, C. (2000) *Making an Impact: Children and Domestic Violence*. London: Jessica Kingsley Publishers.

Pease, A. and B. (1999) *Why Men Don't Listen & Women Can't Read Maps*. Australia: Pease Training International.

Slater-Walker, C. and G. (2002) *An Asperger Marriage*. London: Jessica Kingsley Publishers.

Index